W9-DGH-170

Desserts

Desserts

GALLERY BOOKS
An imprint of W. H. Smith Publishers Inc.
112 Madison Avenue
New York, New York 10016

Editor: Annabel McLaren
Art editor: Caroline Dewing
Production: Richard Churchill
Illustrations and hand lettering: Ian Beck

Published by
GALLERY BOOKS
An imprint of W.H. Smith Publishers Inc.
112 Madison Avenue, New York,
New York 10016

Printed and bound in Italy

ISBN 0 8317 1806-4

Contents

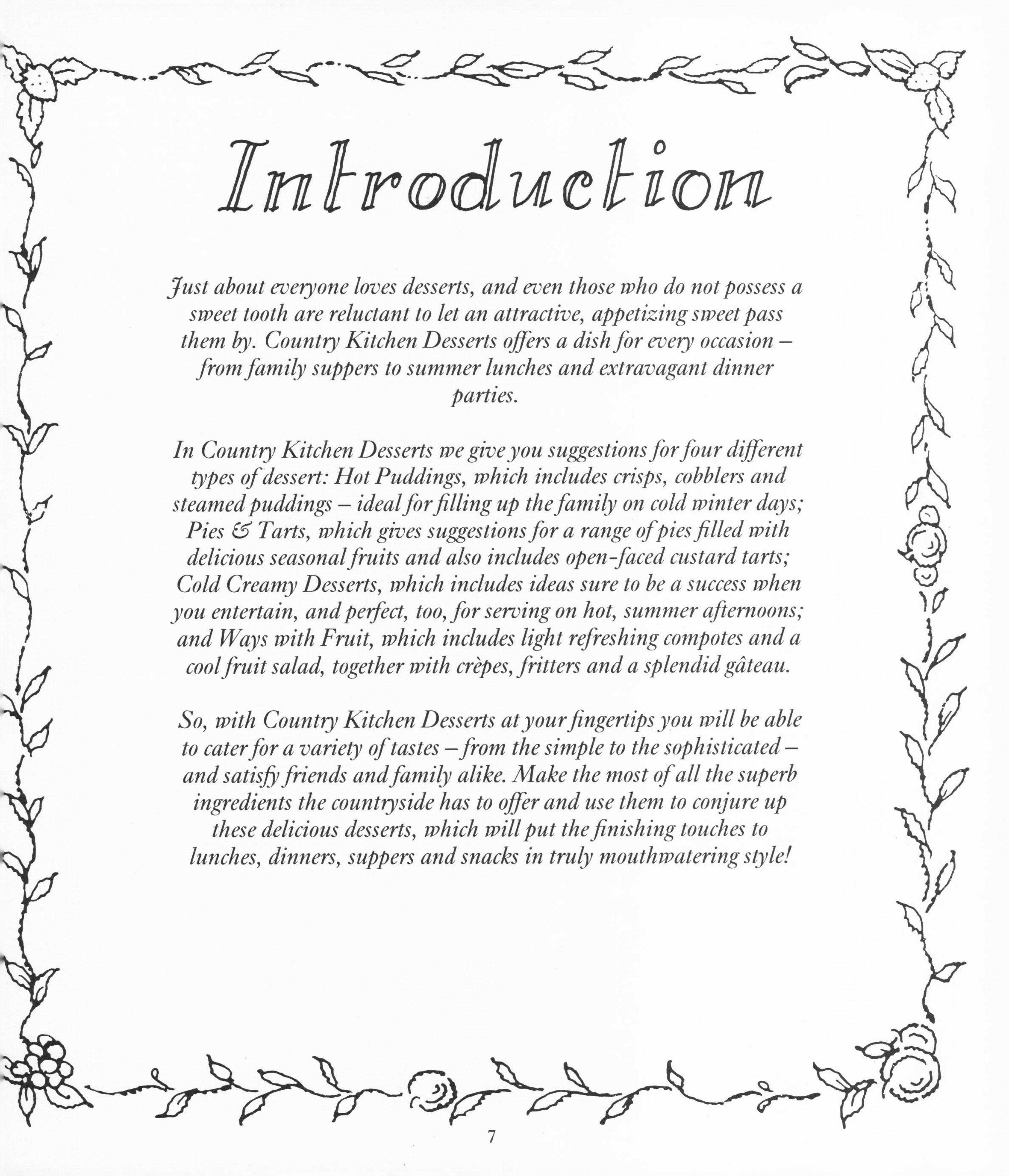

Introduction

Just about everyone loves desserts, and even those who do not possess a sweet tooth are reluctant to let an attractive, appetizing sweet pass them by. Country Kitchen Desserts offers a dish for every occasion – from family suppers to summer lunches and extravagant dinner parties.

In Country Kitchen Desserts we give you suggestions for four different types of dessert: Hot Puddings, which includes crisps, cobblers and steamed puddings – ideal for filling up the family on cold winter days; Pies & Tarts, which gives suggestions for a range of pies filled with delicious seasonal fruits and also includes open-faced custard tarts; Cold Creamy Desserts, which includes ideas sure to be a success when you entertain, and perfect, too, for serving on hot, summer afternoons; and Ways with Fruit, which includes light refreshing compotes and a cool fruit salad, together with crèpes, fritters and a splendid gâteau.

So, with Country Kitchen Desserts at your fingertips you will be able to cater for a variety of tastes – from the simple to the sophisticated – and satisfy friends and family alike. Make the most of all the superb ingredients the countryside has to offer and use them to conjure up these delicious desserts, which will put the finishing touches to lunches, dinners, suppers and snacks in truly mouthwatering style!

Hot Puddings

America's rich culinary heritage owes much to its early settlers. They may have left their homes with little by way of worldly possessions, but in their heads they carried recipes for dishes now popular the world over, including many of these simple yet superb desserts. Their recipes made the most of all the ingredients the New World had to offer: fruits such as tart apples, plums, pears, rhubarb and berries; cereals such as wheat, corn and rice; and the delicious dairy products – milk, cream and eggs. From this homely fare our ancestors conjured some wonderful puddings; why not serve them to your family and friends.

Hot banana crisp

Serves 4–6

3 tablespoons cornstarch
1 tablespoon sugar
1 egg, beaten
2½ cups milk
grated rind of ½ lemon
4 firm bananas
1½ teaspoons lemon juice
TOPPING
¾ cup all-purpose flour
¼ cup diced butter
1 tablespoon sugar
2 tablespoons slivered almonds
2 tablespoons dark brown sugar

1 Preheat the oven to 350°F.

2 In a large bowl mix the cornstarch with the sugar and egg until smooth. Pour the milk into a saucepan, bring almost to a boil and pour onto the cornstarch mixture, stirring well. Return the mixture to the pan and bring to a boil, stirring all the time. Off heat, stir in the lemon rind.

3 Slice the bananas into a 1½ quart pie dish and sprinkle them with the lemon juice. Pour in the prepared sauce, mix lightly but thoroughly together, then level the surface. Place the dish in the oven while you make the topping.

4 Sift the flour into a wide bowl. Cut in the butter and rub it in until the mixture resembles coarse meal, then stir in the sugar.

5 Sprinkle the topping over the banana dessert, covering the surface completely. Scatter the slivered almonds and the brown sugar over the top. Return the dish to the oven and bake for 30 minutes, until the topping is cooked and lightly browned. Serve the dessert immediately, while hot.

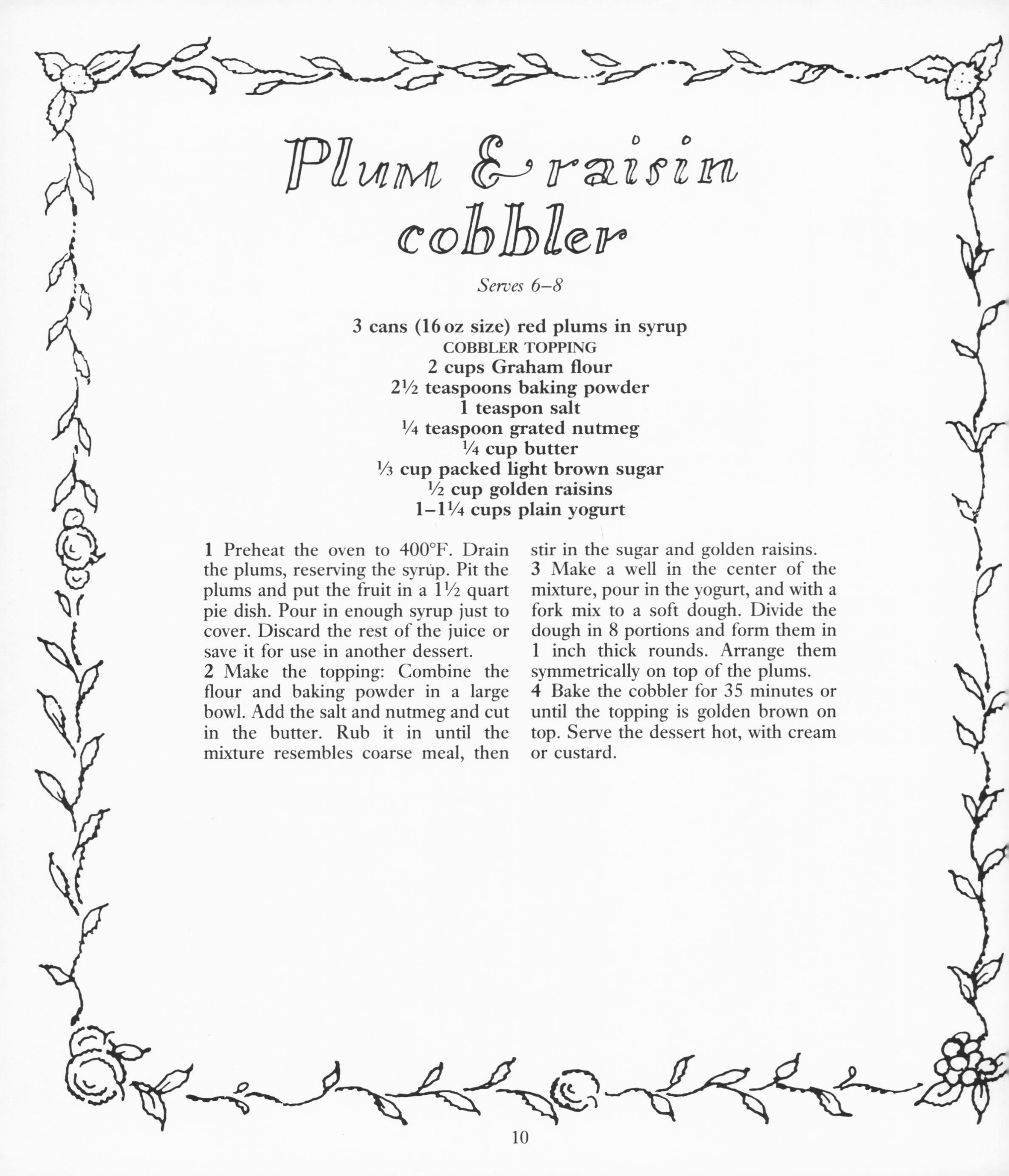

Plum & raisin cobbler

Serves 6–8

3 cans (16 oz size) red plums in syrup
COBBLER TOPPING
2 cups Graham flour
2½ teaspoons baking powder
1 teaspon salt
¼ teaspoon grated nutmeg
¼ cup butter
⅓ cup packed light brown sugar
½ cup golden raisins
1–1¼ cups plain yogurt

1 Preheat the oven to 400°F. Drain the plums, reserving the syrup. Pit the plums and put the fruit in a 1½ quart pie dish. Pour in enough syrup just to cover. Discard the rest of the juice or save it for use in another dessert.

2 Make the topping: Combine the flour and baking powder in a large bowl. Add the salt and nutmeg and cut in the butter. Rub it in until the mixture resembles coarse meal, then stir in the sugar and golden raisins.

3 Make a well in the center of the mixture, pour in the yogurt, and with a fork mix to a soft dough. Divide the dough in 8 portions and form them in 1 inch thick rounds. Arrange them symmetrically on top of the plums.

4 Bake the cobbler for 35 minutes or until the topping is golden brown on top. Serve the dessert hot, with cream or custard.

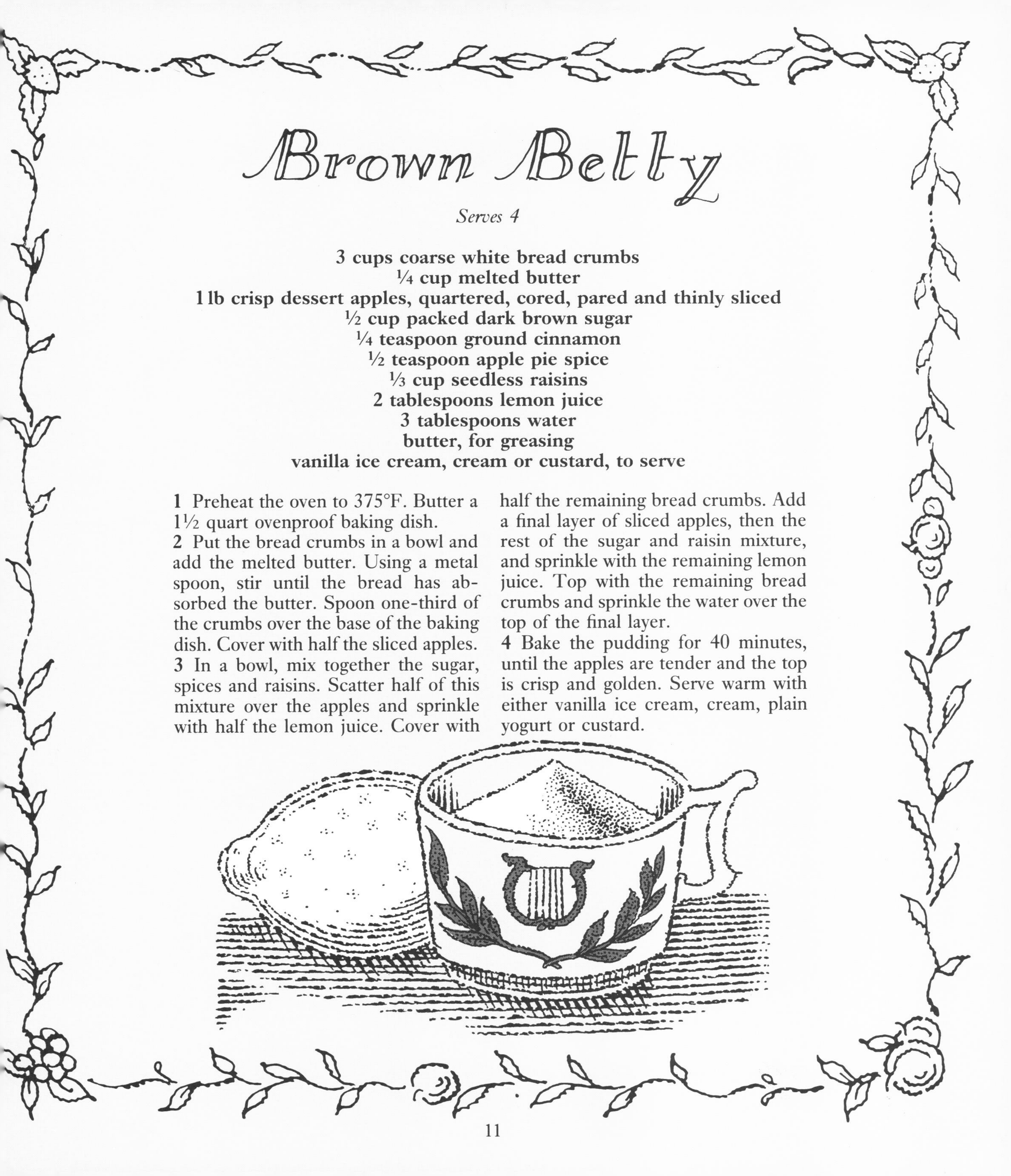

Brown Betty

Serves 4

3 cups coarse white bread crumbs
¼ cup melted butter
1 lb crisp dessert apples, quartered, cored, pared and thinly sliced
½ cup packed dark brown sugar
¼ teaspoon ground cinnamon
½ teaspoon apple pie spice
⅓ cup seedless raisins
2 tablespoons lemon juice
3 tablespoons water
butter, for greasing
vanilla ice cream, cream or custard, to serve

1 Preheat the oven to 375°F. Butter a 1½ quart ovenproof baking dish.
2 Put the bread crumbs in a bowl and add the melted butter. Using a metal spoon, stir until the bread has absorbed the butter. Spoon one-third of the crumbs over the base of the baking dish. Cover with half the sliced apples.
3 In a bowl, mix together the sugar, spices and raisins. Scatter half of this mixture over the apples and sprinkle with half the lemon juice. Cover with half the remaining bread crumbs. Add a final layer of sliced apples, then the rest of the sugar and raisin mixture, and sprinkle with the remaining lemon juice. Top with the remaining bread crumbs and sprinkle the water over the top of the final layer.
4 Bake the pudding for 40 minutes, until the apples are tender and the top is crisp and golden. Serve warm with either vanilla ice cream, cream, plain yogurt or custard.

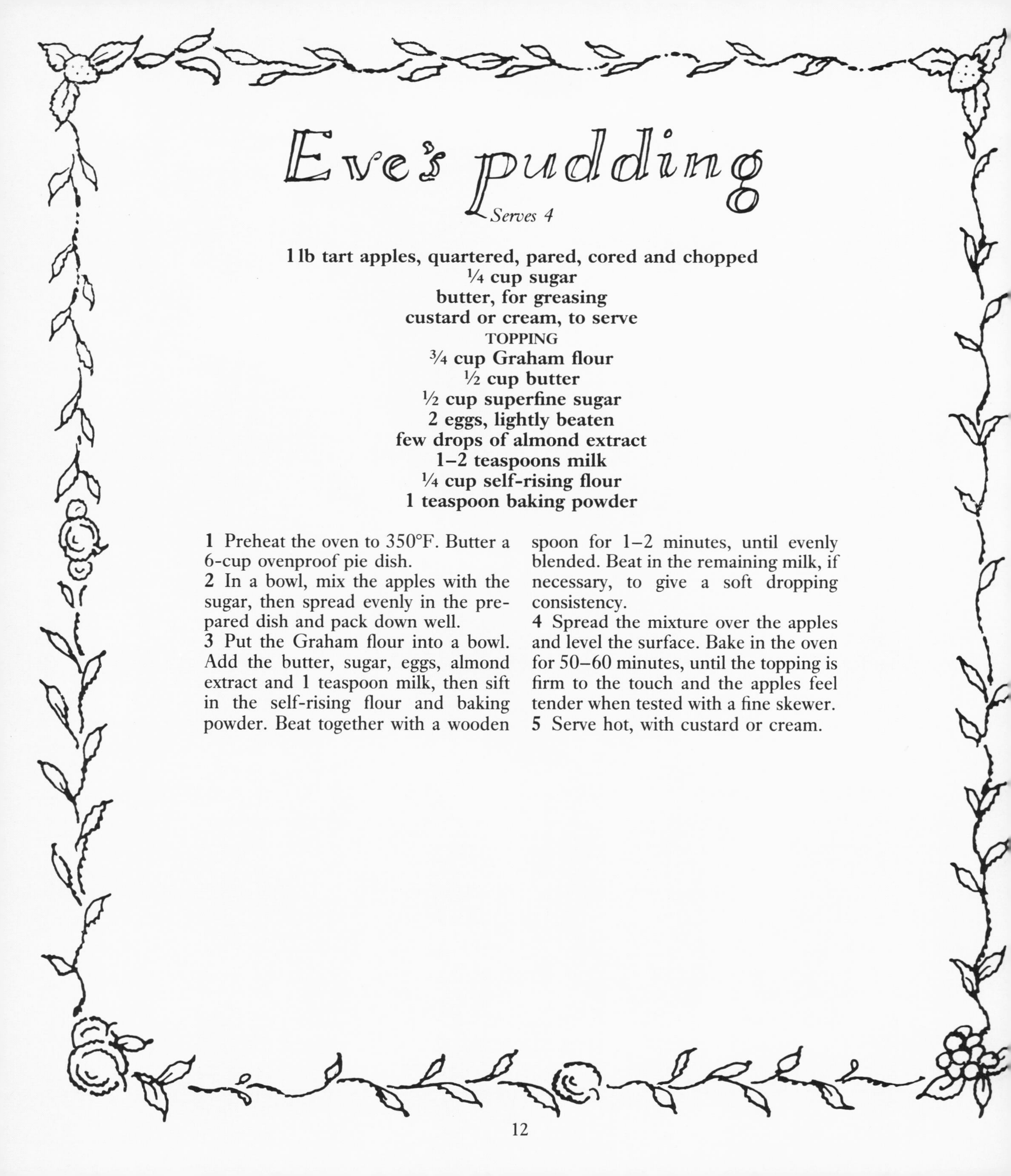

Eve's pudding

Serves 4

1 lb tart apples, quartered, pared, cored and chopped
¼ cup sugar
butter, for greasing
custard or cream, to serve

TOPPING

¾ cup Graham flour
½ cup butter
½ cup superfine sugar
2 eggs, lightly beaten
few drops of almond extract
1–2 teaspoons milk
¼ cup self-rising flour
1 teaspoon baking powder

1 Preheat the oven to 350°F. Butter a 6-cup ovenproof pie dish.
2 In a bowl, mix the apples with the sugar, then spread evenly in the prepared dish and pack down well.
3 Put the Graham flour into a bowl. Add the butter, sugar, eggs, almond extract and 1 teaspoon milk, then sift in the self-rising flour and baking powder. Beat together with a wooden spoon for 1–2 minutes, until evenly blended. Beat in the remaining milk, if necessary, to give a soft dropping consistency.
4 Spread the mixture over the apples and level the surface. Bake in the oven for 50–60 minutes, until the topping is firm to the touch and the apples feel tender when tested with a fine skewer.
5 Serve hot, with custard or cream.

Old-fashioned bread & butter pudding

Serves 4

4 medium thick slices white bread, crusts removed
3 tablespoons butter
⅓ cup golden raisins
2 tablespoons superfine sugar
2 large eggs
1¼ cups milk
¼ teaspoon freshly grated nutmeg

1 Butter the bread well on one side. Cut each slice into 4.
2 Layer bread, buttered side up, in a well-greased 3-cup ovenproof dish, sprinkling golden raisins and sugar between each layer and on top.
3 In a bowl, beat the eggs and milk together and strain over the bread. Let stand in a cool place for 30 minutes.
4 Preheat the oven to 350°F.
5 Sprinkle the nutmeg over the pudding and bake in the oven for 25–30 minutes until set and golden brown. Serve hot.

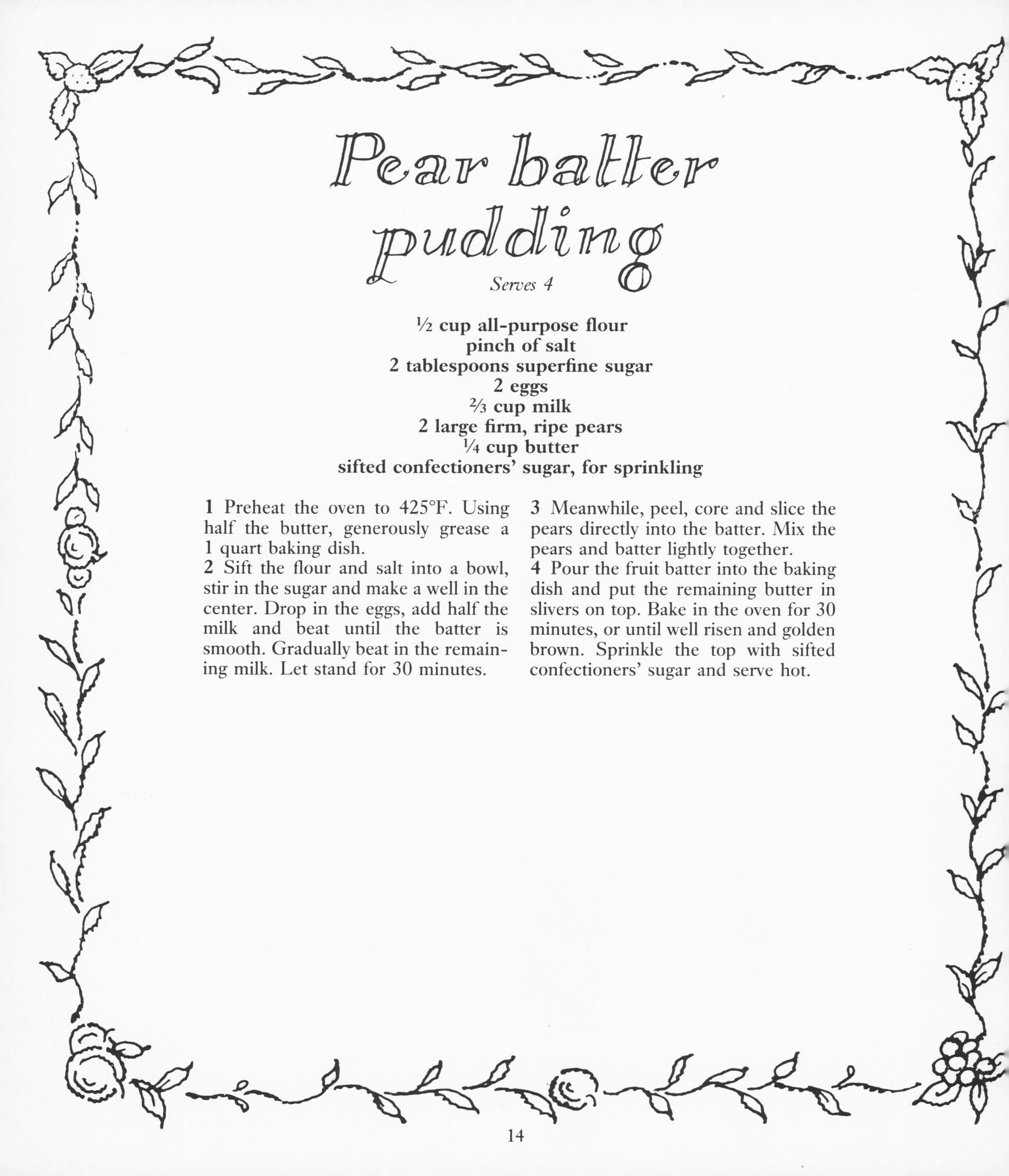

Pear batter pudding

Serves 4

½ cup all-purpose flour
pinch of salt
2 tablespoons superfine sugar
2 eggs
⅔ cup milk
2 large firm, ripe pears
¼ cup butter
sifted confectioners' sugar, for sprinkling

1 Preheat the oven to 425°F. Using half the butter, generously grease a 1 quart baking dish.
2 Sift the flour and salt into a bowl, stir in the sugar and make a well in the center. Drop in the eggs, add half the milk and beat until the batter is smooth. Gradually beat in the remaining milk. Let stand for 30 minutes.
3 Meanwhile, peel, core and slice the pears directly into the batter. Mix the pears and batter lightly together.
4 Pour the fruit batter into the baking dish and put the remaining butter in slivers on top. Bake in the oven for 30 minutes, or until well risen and golden brown. Sprinkle the top with sifted confectioners' sugar and serve hot.

Rhubarb oatmeal crunch

Serves 4

1½ lb rhubarb
½ cup superfine sugar
1 tablespoon orange juice
heavy cream, chilled, to serve
TOPPING
1 cup all-purpose flour
¼ cup butter
3 tablespoons superfine sugar
3 tablespoons medium oatmeal
1 tablespoon dark brown sugar

1 Trim and wash the rhubarb. Cut it in 1 inch lengths and put it in a 1½ quart ovenproof dish. Sprinkle with the superfine sugar and orange juice.
2 Preheat the oven to 400°F.
3 Make the topping: Put the flour into a large bowl, cut in the butter and rub it in until the mixture resembles coarse meal. Stir in the superfine sugar.
4 Sprinkle the mixture over the rhubarb.
5 In a bowl, mix together the oatmeal and brown sugar and sprinkle on top of the pudding.
6 Put in the oven and bake for 45 minutes until the topping is golden brown. Serve immediately with chilled heavy cream.

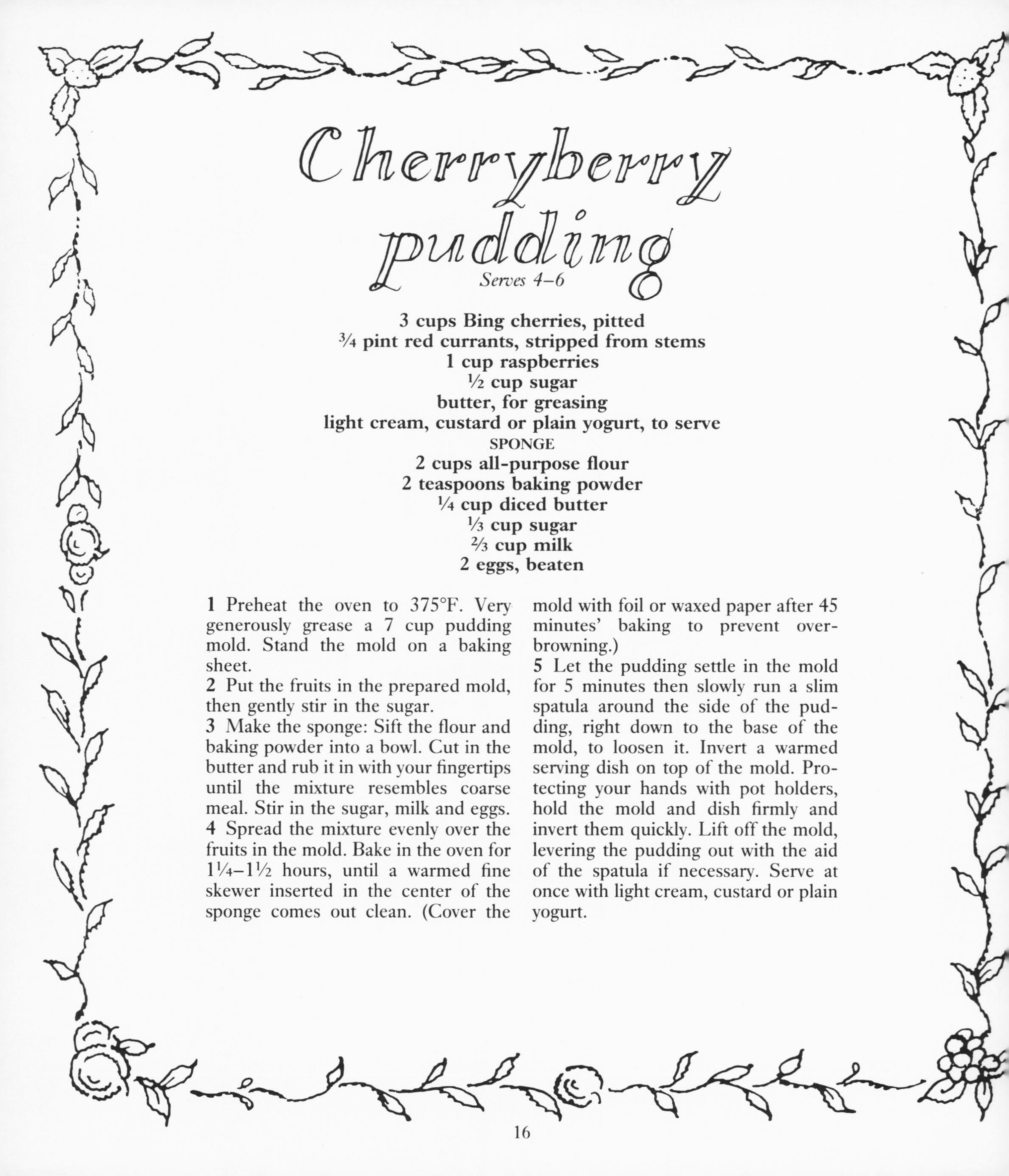

Cherryberry pudding

Serves 4–6

3 cups Bing cherries, pitted
¾ pint red currants, stripped from stems
1 cup raspberries
½ cup sugar
butter, for greasing
light cream, custard or plain yogurt, to serve

SPONGE

2 cups all-purpose flour
2 teaspoons baking powder
¼ cup diced butter
⅓ cup sugar
⅔ cup milk
2 eggs, beaten

1 Preheat the oven to 375°F. Very generously grease a 7 cup pudding mold. Stand the mold on a baking sheet.
2 Put the fruits in the prepared mold, then gently stir in the sugar.
3 Make the sponge: Sift the flour and baking powder into a bowl. Cut in the butter and rub it in with your fingertips until the mixture resembles coarse meal. Stir in the sugar, milk and eggs.
4 Spread the mixture evenly over the fruits in the mold. Bake in the oven for 1¼–1½ hours, until a warmed fine skewer inserted in the center of the sponge comes out clean. (Cover the mold with foil or waxed paper after 45 minutes' baking to prevent over-browning.)
5 Let the pudding settle in the mold for 5 minutes then slowly run a slim spatula around the side of the pudding, right down to the base of the mold, to loosen it. Invert a warmed serving dish on top of the mold. Protecting your hands with pot holders, hold the mold and dish firmly and invert them quickly. Lift off the mold, levering the pudding out with the aid of the spatula if necessary. Serve at once with light cream, custard or plain yogurt.

Rich rice pudding

Serves 4

½ cup uncooked short-grain rice (not converted)
2½ cups milk
finely grated rind of ½ orange
⅓ cup superfine sugar
2 tablespoons butter
3 egg yolks, beaten
⅔ cup light cream
butter, for greasing
red jam, to serve

1 Preheat the oven to 350°F and generously butter a deep 1½ quart ovenproof dish.
2 Put the rice in a saucepan with milk and orange rind and bring slowly to a boil. Cook, stirring occasionally, for 15–20 minutes, until just tender.
3 Off heat, add the superfine sugar and butter and stir until melted. Let the rice mixture cool for 5 minutes. Thoroughly stir in the beaten egg yolks, followed by the cream.
4 Pour into the prepared dish and bake in the oven for about 40 minutes, stirring thoroughly three times during cooking. At the end of cooking the pudding will have a thin skin and most of the liquid will have been absorbed. Serve warm, topped with red jam or stewed fruit.

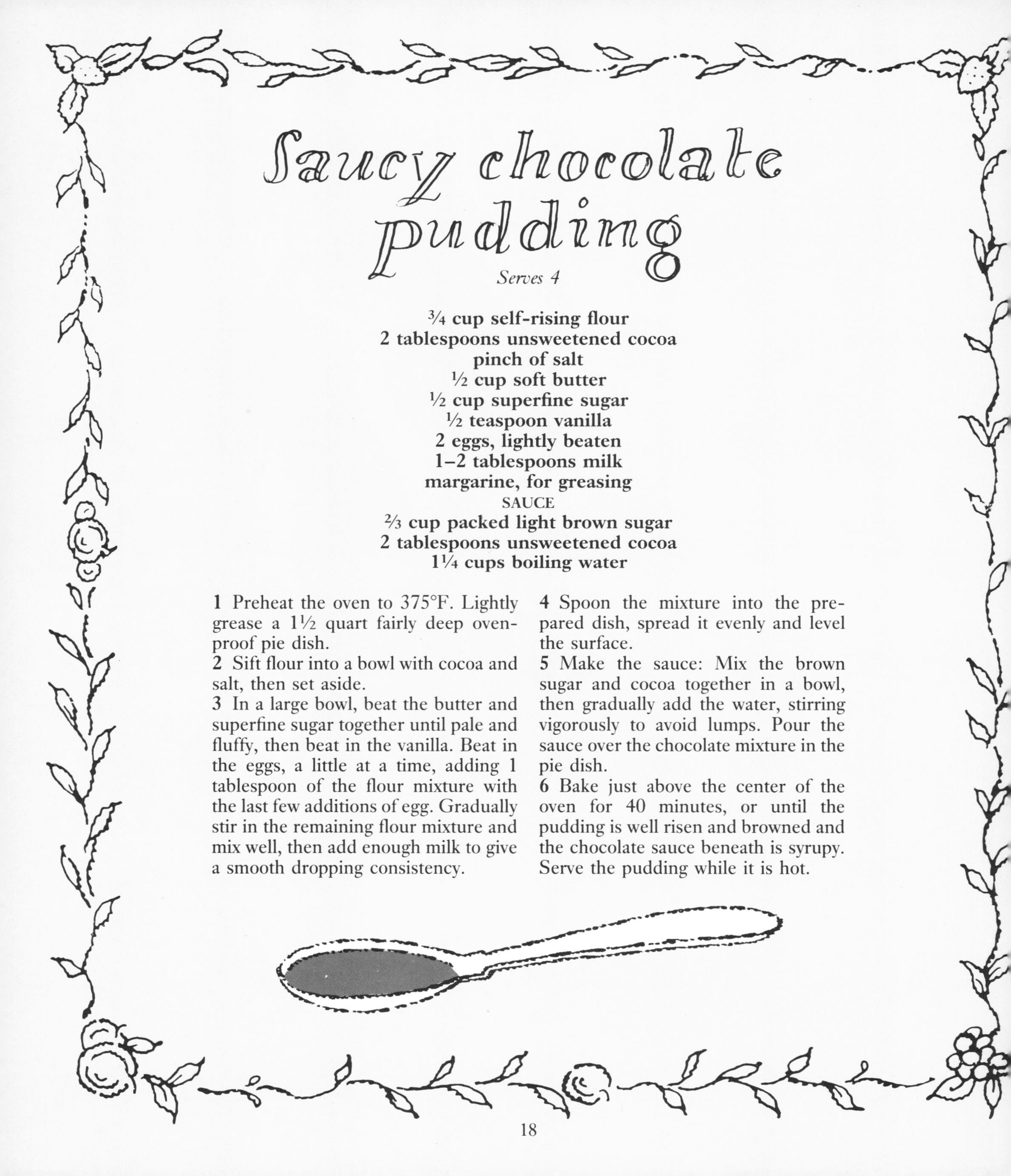

Saucy chocolate pudding

Serves 4

¾ cup self-rising flour
2 tablespoons unsweetened cocoa
pinch of salt
½ cup soft butter
½ cup superfine sugar
½ teaspoon vanilla
2 eggs, lightly beaten
1–2 tablespoons milk
margarine, for greasing
SAUCE
⅔ cup packed light brown sugar
2 tablespoons unsweetened cocoa
1¼ cups boiling water

1 Preheat the oven to 375°F. Lightly grease a 1½ quart fairly deep oven-proof pie dish.

2 Sift flour into a bowl with cocoa and salt, then set aside.

3 In a large bowl, beat the butter and superfine sugar together until pale and fluffy, then beat in the vanilla. Beat in the eggs, a little at a time, adding 1 tablespoon of the flour mixture with the last few additions of egg. Gradually stir in the remaining flour mixture and mix well, then add enough milk to give a smooth dropping consistency.

4 Spoon the mixture into the prepared dish, spread it evenly and level the surface.

5 Make the sauce: Mix the brown sugar and cocoa together in a bowl, then gradually add the water, stirring vigorously to avoid lumps. Pour the sauce over the chocolate mixture in the pie dish.

6 Bake just above the center of the oven for 40 minutes, or until the pudding is well risen and browned and the chocolate sauce beneath is syrupy. Serve the pudding while it is hot.

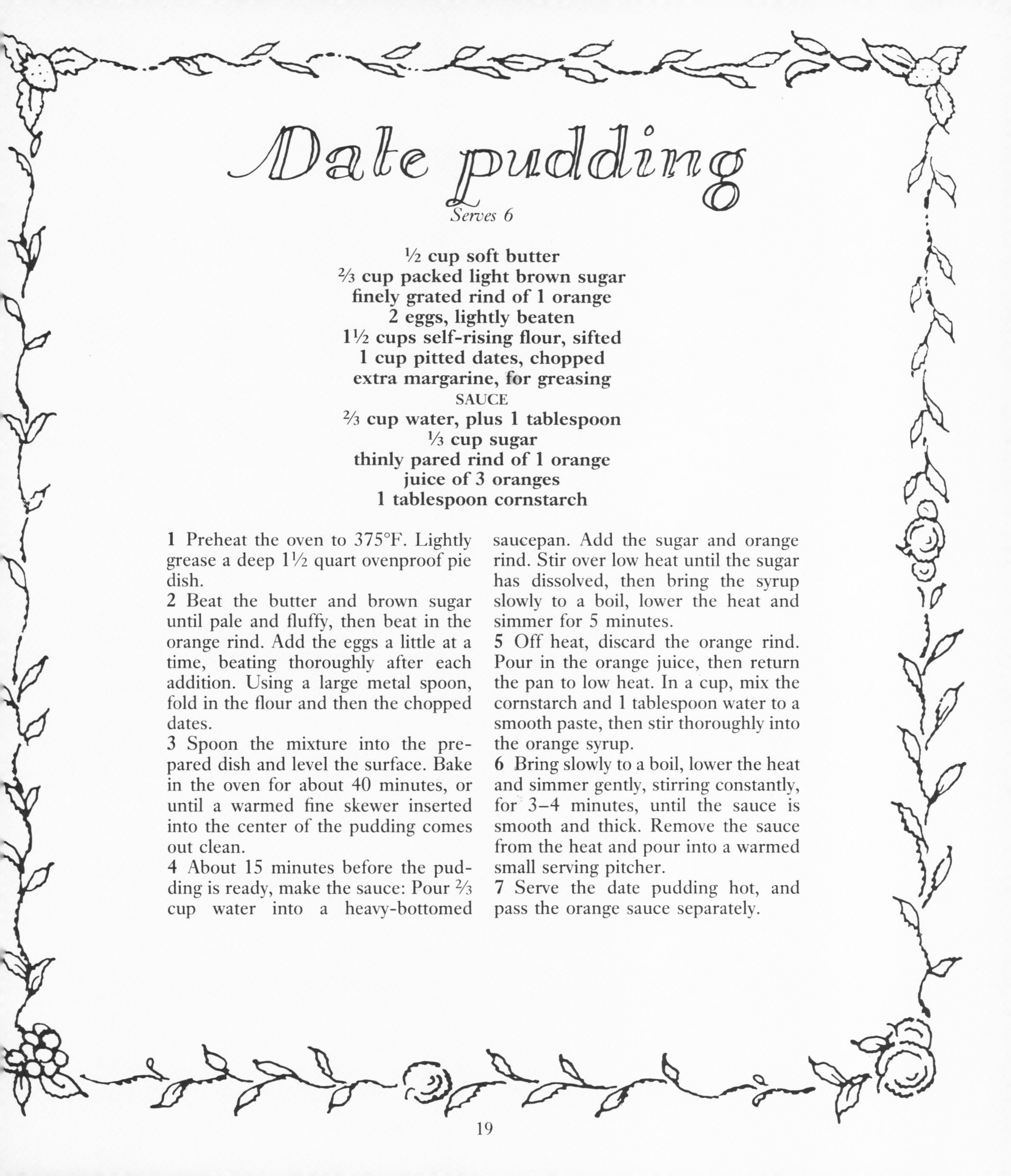

Date pudding

Serves 6

½ cup soft butter
⅔ cup packed light brown sugar
finely grated rind of 1 orange
2 eggs, lightly beaten
1½ cups self-rising flour, sifted
1 cup pitted dates, chopped
extra margarine, for greasing

SAUCE

⅔ cup water, plus 1 tablespoon
⅓ cup sugar
thinly pared rind of 1 orange
juice of 3 oranges
1 tablespoon cornstarch

1 Preheat the oven to 375°F. Lightly grease a deep 1½ quart ovenproof pie dish.

2 Beat the butter and brown sugar until pale and fluffy, then beat in the orange rind. Add the eggs a little at a time, beating thoroughly after each addition. Using a large metal spoon, fold in the flour and then the chopped dates.

3 Spoon the mixture into the prepared dish and level the surface. Bake in the oven for about 40 minutes, or until a warmed fine skewer inserted into the center of the pudding comes out clean.

4 About 15 minutes before the pudding is ready, make the sauce: Pour ⅔ cup water into a heavy-bottomed saucepan. Add the sugar and orange rind. Stir over low heat until the sugar has dissolved, then bring the syrup slowly to a boil, lower the heat and simmer for 5 minutes.

5 Off heat, discard the orange rind. Pour in the orange juice, then return the pan to low heat. In a cup, mix the cornstarch and 1 tablespoon water to a smooth paste, then stir thoroughly into the orange syrup.

6 Bring slowly to a boil, lower the heat and simmer gently, stirring constantly, for 3–4 minutes, until the sauce is smooth and thick. Remove the sauce from the heat and pour into a warmed small serving pitcher.

7 Serve the date pudding hot, and pass the orange sauce separately.

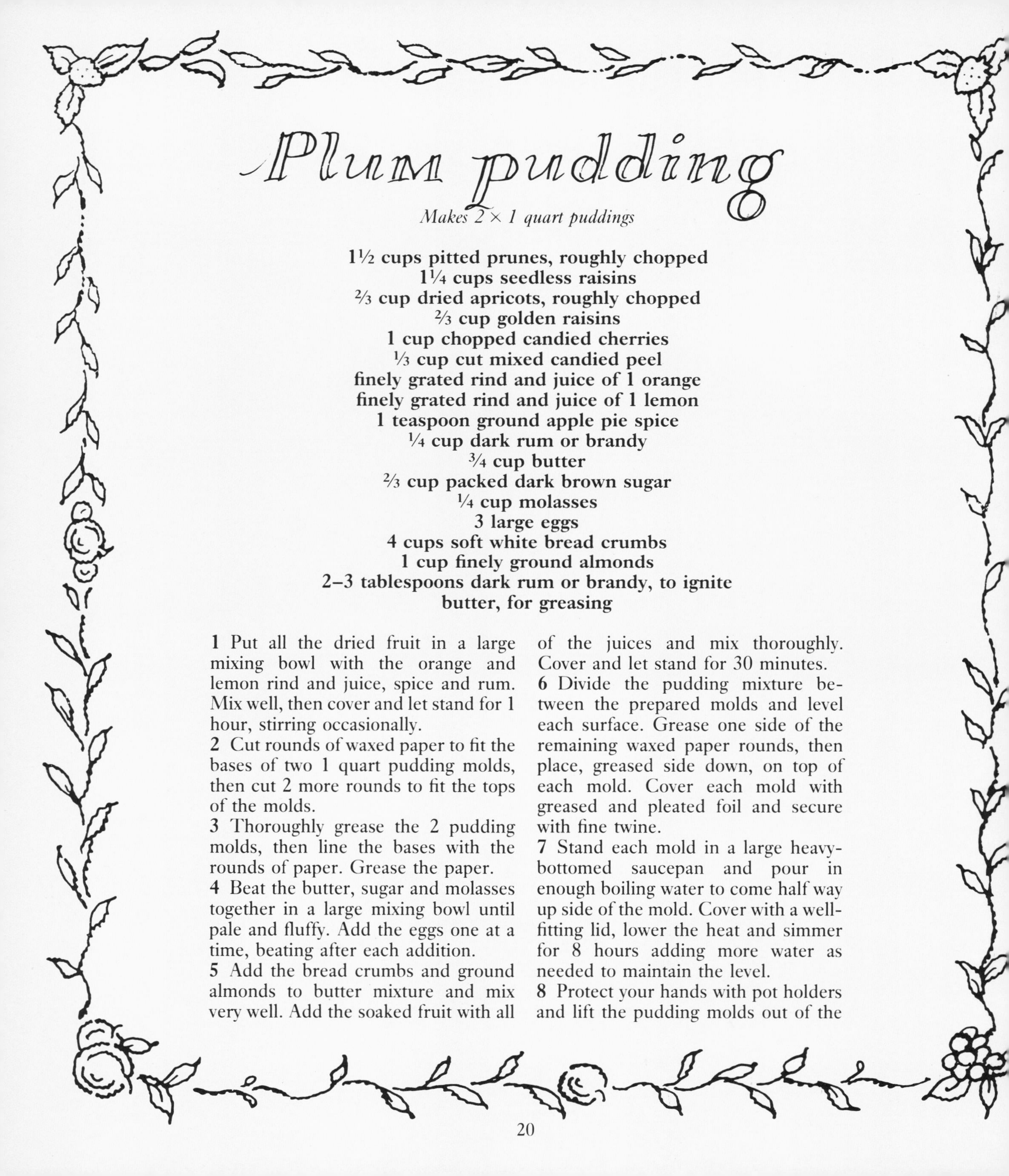

Plum pudding

Makes 2 × 1 quart puddings

1½ cups pitted prunes, roughly chopped
1¼ cups seedless raisins
⅔ cup dried apricots, roughly chopped
⅔ cup golden raisins
1 cup chopped candied cherries
⅓ cup cut mixed candied peel
finely grated rind and juice of 1 orange
finely grated rind and juice of 1 lemon
1 teaspoon ground apple pie spice
¼ cup dark rum or brandy
¾ cup butter
⅔ cup packed dark brown sugar
¼ cup molasses
3 large eggs
4 cups soft white bread crumbs
1 cup finely ground almonds
2–3 tablespoons dark rum or brandy, to ignite
butter, for greasing

1 Put all the dried fruit in a large mixing bowl with the orange and lemon rind and juice, spice and rum. Mix well, then cover and let stand for 1 hour, stirring occasionally.

2 Cut rounds of waxed paper to fit the bases of two 1 quart pudding molds, then cut 2 more rounds to fit the tops of the molds.

3 Thoroughly grease the 2 pudding molds, then line the bases with the rounds of paper. Grease the paper.

4 Beat the butter, sugar and molasses together in a large mixing bowl until pale and fluffy. Add the eggs one at a time, beating after each addition.

5 Add the bread crumbs and ground almonds to butter mixture and mix very well. Add the soaked fruit with all of the juices and mix thoroughly. Cover and let stand for 30 minutes.

6 Divide the pudding mixture between the prepared molds and level each surface. Grease one side of the remaining waxed paper rounds, then place, greased side down, on top of each mold. Cover each mold with greased and pleated foil and secure with fine twine.

7 Stand each mold in a large heavy-bottomed saucepan and pour in enough boiling water to come half way up side of the mold. Cover with a well-fitting lid, lower the heat and simmer for 8 hours adding more water as needed to maintain the level.

8 Protect your hands with pot holders and lift the pudding molds out of the pans and remove the foil. Cover with clean dish towels and let cool. When cold, re-cover with clean foil and store puddings in a cool dry airy place.

9 To serve: Reheat for 2–3 hours as in stage 7. Lift pudding molds out of pans and remove foil and waxed paper coverings. Invert on a warmed serving platter and remove paper linings.

10 To blaze puddings: Put the rum into a cup, then stand the cup in a bowl of hot water to warm the spirit. Pour the warmed spirit over the pudding and ignite. Take the pudding to the table at once, while still alight, and serve as soon as all the flames have died down. Pass brandy butter separately (recipe follows).

Brandy butter

Serves 6–8

⅓ cup soft butter
1 cup confectioners' sugar, sifted
1–2 tablespoons brandy

1 In a large bowl, beat the butter with a wooden spoon until creamy.

2 Beat in the sugar until it is well mixed and thick and smooth, then gradually beat in brandy to taste.

3 Transfer the butter to a serving bowl and pat it into the desired shape. Rough up the surface with a fork, then chill in the refrigerator for at least 2 hours before serving.

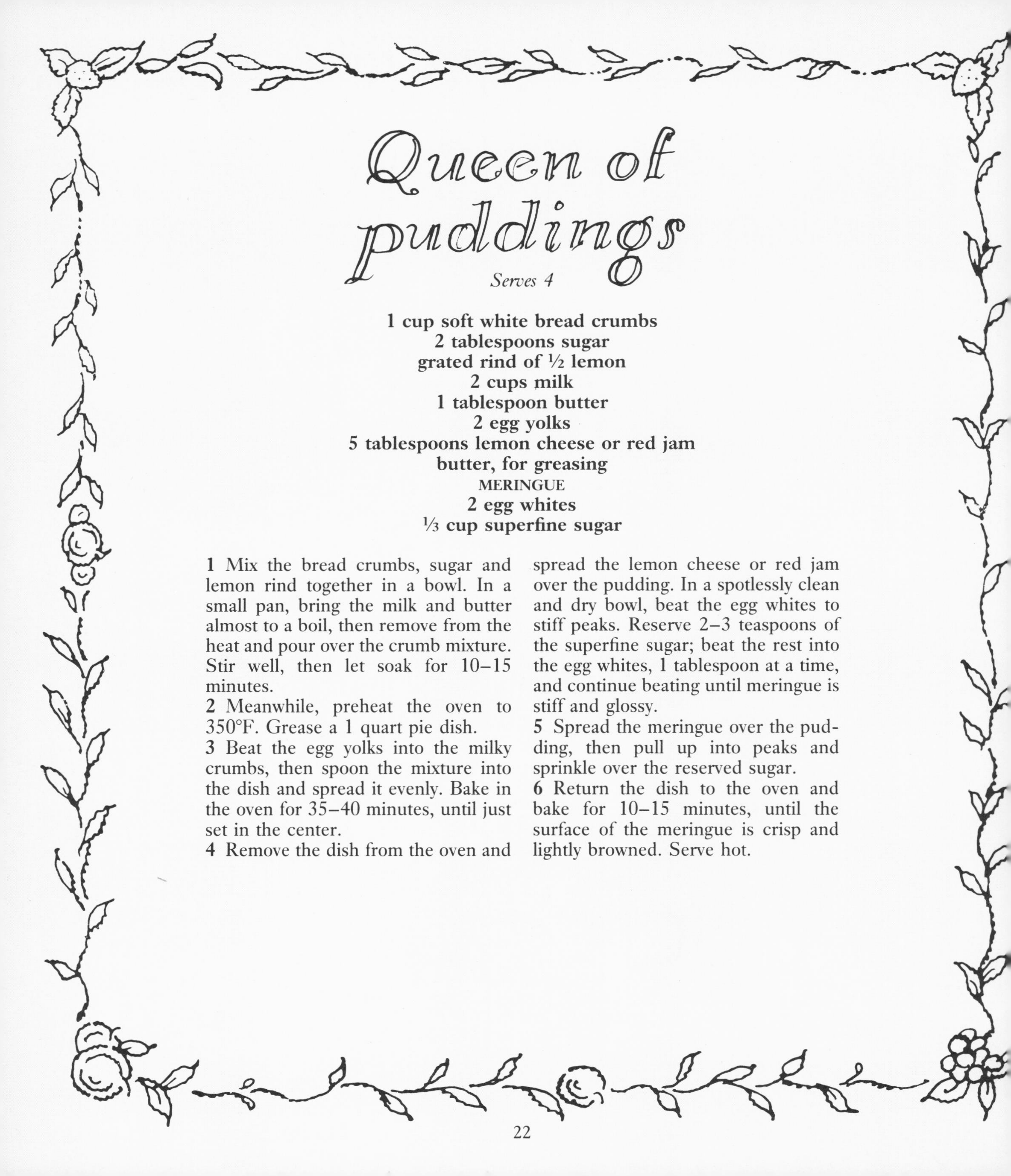

Queen of puddings

Serves 4

1 cup soft white bread crumbs
2 tablespoons sugar
grated rind of ½ lemon
2 cups milk
1 tablespoon butter
2 egg yolks
5 tablespoons lemon cheese or red jam
butter, for greasing
MERINGUE
2 egg whites
⅓ cup superfine sugar

1 Mix the bread crumbs, sugar and lemon rind together in a bowl. In a small pan, bring the milk and butter almost to a boil, then remove from the heat and pour over the crumb mixture. Stir well, then let soak for 10–15 minutes.
2 Meanwhile, preheat the oven to 350°F. Grease a 1 quart pie dish.
3 Beat the egg yolks into the milky crumbs, then spoon the mixture into the dish and spread it evenly. Bake in the oven for 35–40 minutes, until just set in the center.
4 Remove the dish from the oven and spread the lemon cheese or red jam over the pudding. In a spotlessly clean and dry bowl, beat the egg whites to stiff peaks. Reserve 2–3 teaspoons of the superfine sugar; beat the rest into the egg whites, 1 tablespoon at a time, and continue beating until meringue is stiff and glossy.
5 Spread the meringue over the pudding, then pull up into peaks and sprinkle over the reserved sugar.
6 Return the dish to the oven and bake for 10–15 minutes, until the surface of the meringue is crisp and lightly browned. Serve hot.

Peanut butter pudding

Serves 4

1½ cups all-purpose flour
1½ teaspoons baking powder
¼ cup soft margarine
⅓ cup crunchy peanut butter
finely grated rind of 1 orange
½ cup packed light brown sugar
2 eggs, beaten
¼ cup orange juice
3 tablespoons milk
soft margarine, for greasing

1 Preheat the oven to 350°F. Thoroughly grease a 1½ quart ovenproof pie dish.
2 Sift the flour and baking powder into a bowl and reserve.
3 In a separate bowl, beat the margarine, peanut butter, orange rind and sugar together until pale and fluffy. Add the eggs, a little at a time, beating very thoroughly after each addition until well mixed.
4 Using a large metal spoon, fold in the sifted flour alternately with the orange juice. Add the milk and mix well, then spoon the mixture into the prepared dish and level the surface with the back of a spoon.
5 Bake the pudding in the oven for about 45 minutes, or until just firm to the touch in the center. (The top may crack slightly.) Serve the pudding hot with cream or vanilla sauce.

Pies & Tarts

When the trees are laden with ripe, golden fruit every country cook's thoughts turn to tarts and pies – the ideal culinary solution for dealing with a glut of seasonal fruit. You can either use produce from your own garden, or buy cheaply in the markets; if you take advantage of abundance in the fall you can freeze a selection of pies and tarts for later in the year. In this chapter we give you suggestions for fruit pies with a range of delicious fillings – from dessert apples to oranges and grapefruit, blueberries and cranberries and even tropical fruit such as mangoes. There are also recipes for open-faced tarts with creamy custard fillings, together with clear directions for making both sweet pie and cream cheese dough.

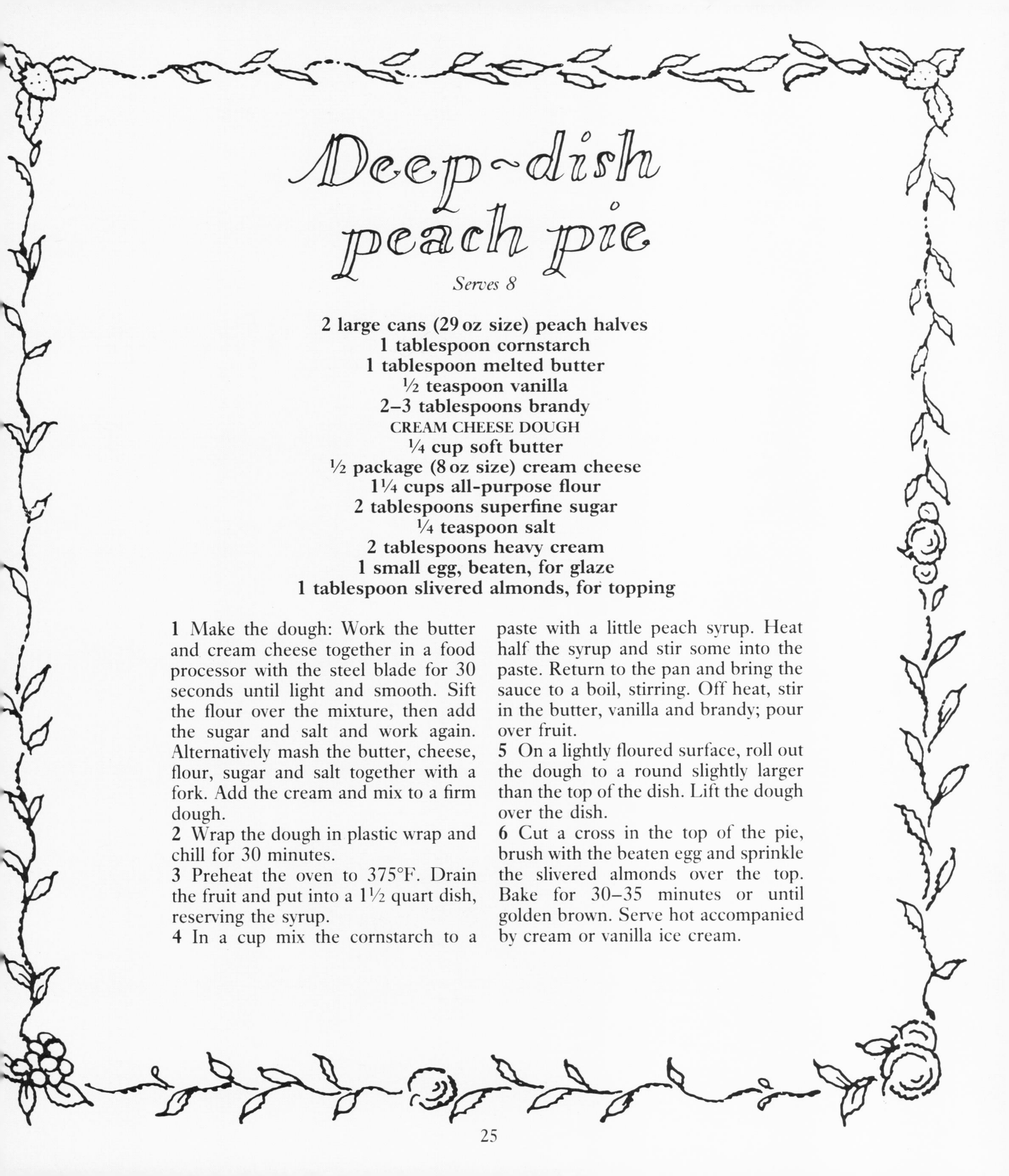

Deep-dish peach pie

Serves 8

2 large cans (29 oz size) peach halves
1 tablespoon cornstarch
1 tablespoon melted butter
½ teaspoon vanilla
2–3 tablespoons brandy
CREAM CHEESE DOUGH
¼ cup soft butter
½ package (8 oz size) cream cheese
1¼ cups all-purpose flour
2 tablespoons superfine sugar
¼ teaspoon salt
2 tablespoons heavy cream
1 small egg, beaten, for glaze
1 tablespoon slivered almonds, for topping

1 Make the dough: Work the butter and cream cheese together in a food processor with the steel blade for 30 seconds until light and smooth. Sift the flour over the mixture, then add the sugar and salt and work again. Alternatively mash the butter, cheese, flour, sugar and salt together with a fork. Add the cream and mix to a firm dough.

2 Wrap the dough in plastic wrap and chill for 30 minutes.

3 Preheat the oven to 375°F. Drain the fruit and put into a 1½ quart dish, reserving the syrup.

4 In a cup mix the cornstarch to a paste with a little peach syrup. Heat half the syrup and stir some into the paste. Return to the pan and bring the sauce to a boil, stirring. Off heat, stir in the butter, vanilla and brandy; pour over fruit.

5 On a lightly floured surface, roll out the dough to a round slightly larger than the top of the dish. Lift the dough over the dish.

6 Cut a cross in the top of the pie, brush with the beaten egg and sprinkle the slivered almonds over the top. Bake for 30–35 minutes or until golden brown. Serve hot accompanied by cream or vanilla ice cream.

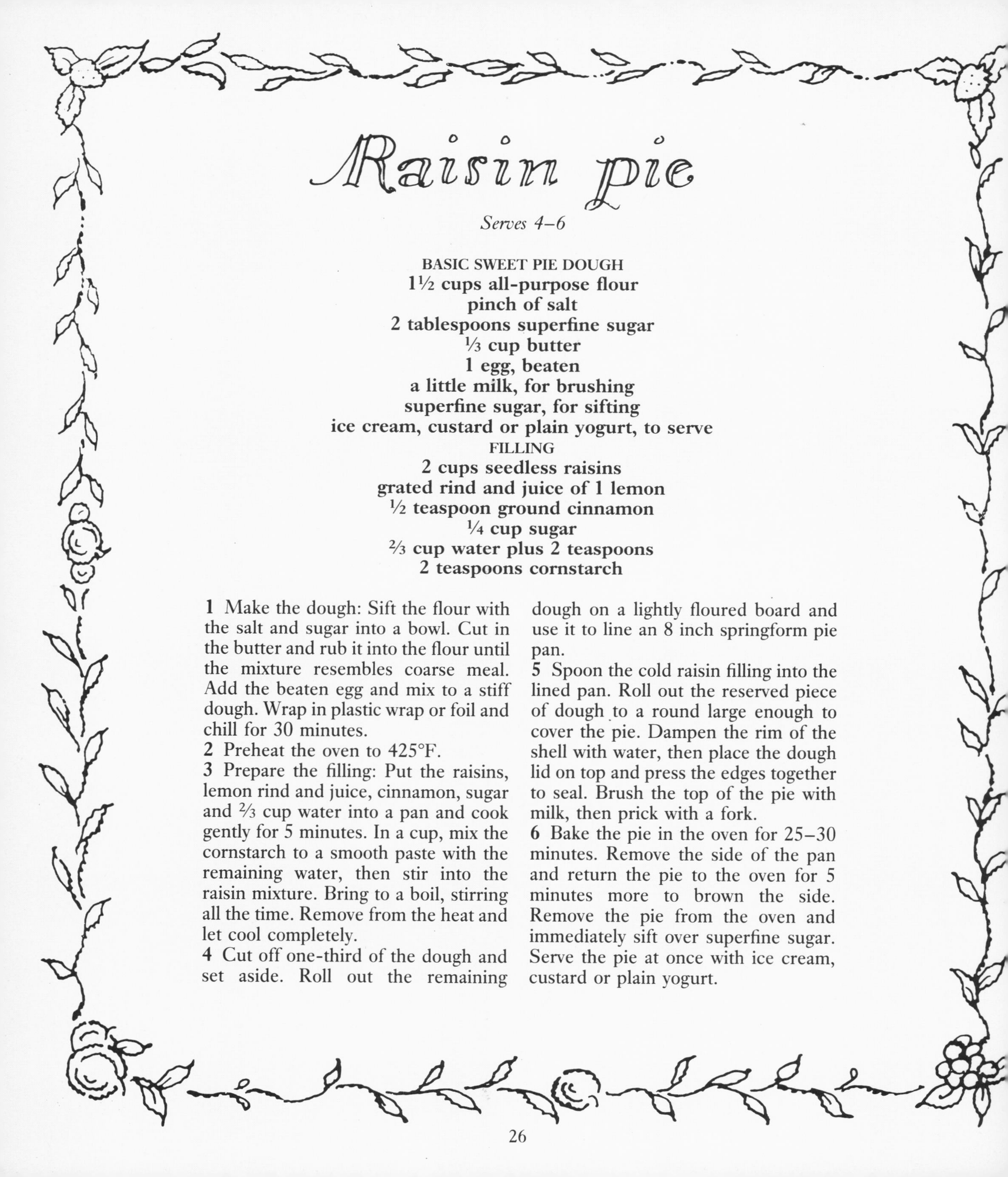

Raisin pie

Serves 4–6

BASIC SWEET PIE DOUGH
1½ cups all-purpose flour
pinch of salt
2 tablespoons superfine sugar
⅓ cup butter
1 egg, beaten
a little milk, for brushing
superfine sugar, for sifting
ice cream, custard or plain yogurt, to serve

FILLING
2 cups seedless raisins
grated rind and juice of 1 lemon
½ teaspoon ground cinnamon
¼ cup sugar
⅔ cup water plus 2 teaspoons
2 teaspoons cornstarch

1 Make the dough: Sift the flour with the salt and sugar into a bowl. Cut in the butter and rub it into the flour until the mixture resembles coarse meal. Add the beaten egg and mix to a stiff dough. Wrap in plastic wrap or foil and chill for 30 minutes.
2 Preheat the oven to 425°F.
3 Prepare the filling: Put the raisins, lemon rind and juice, cinnamon, sugar and ⅔ cup water into a pan and cook gently for 5 minutes. In a cup, mix the cornstarch to a smooth paste with the remaining water, then stir into the raisin mixture. Bring to a boil, stirring all the time. Remove from the heat and let cool completely.
4 Cut off one-third of the dough and set aside. Roll out the remaining dough on a lightly floured board and use it to line an 8 inch springform pie pan.
5 Spoon the cold raisin filling into the lined pan. Roll out the reserved piece of dough to a round large enough to cover the pie. Dampen the rim of the shell with water, then place the dough lid on top and press the edges together to seal. Brush the top of the pie with milk, then prick with a fork.
6 Bake the pie in the oven for 25–30 minutes. Remove the side of the pan and return the pie to the oven for 5 minutes more to brown the side. Remove the pie from the oven and immediately sift over superfine sugar. Serve the pie at once with ice cream, custard or plain yogurt.

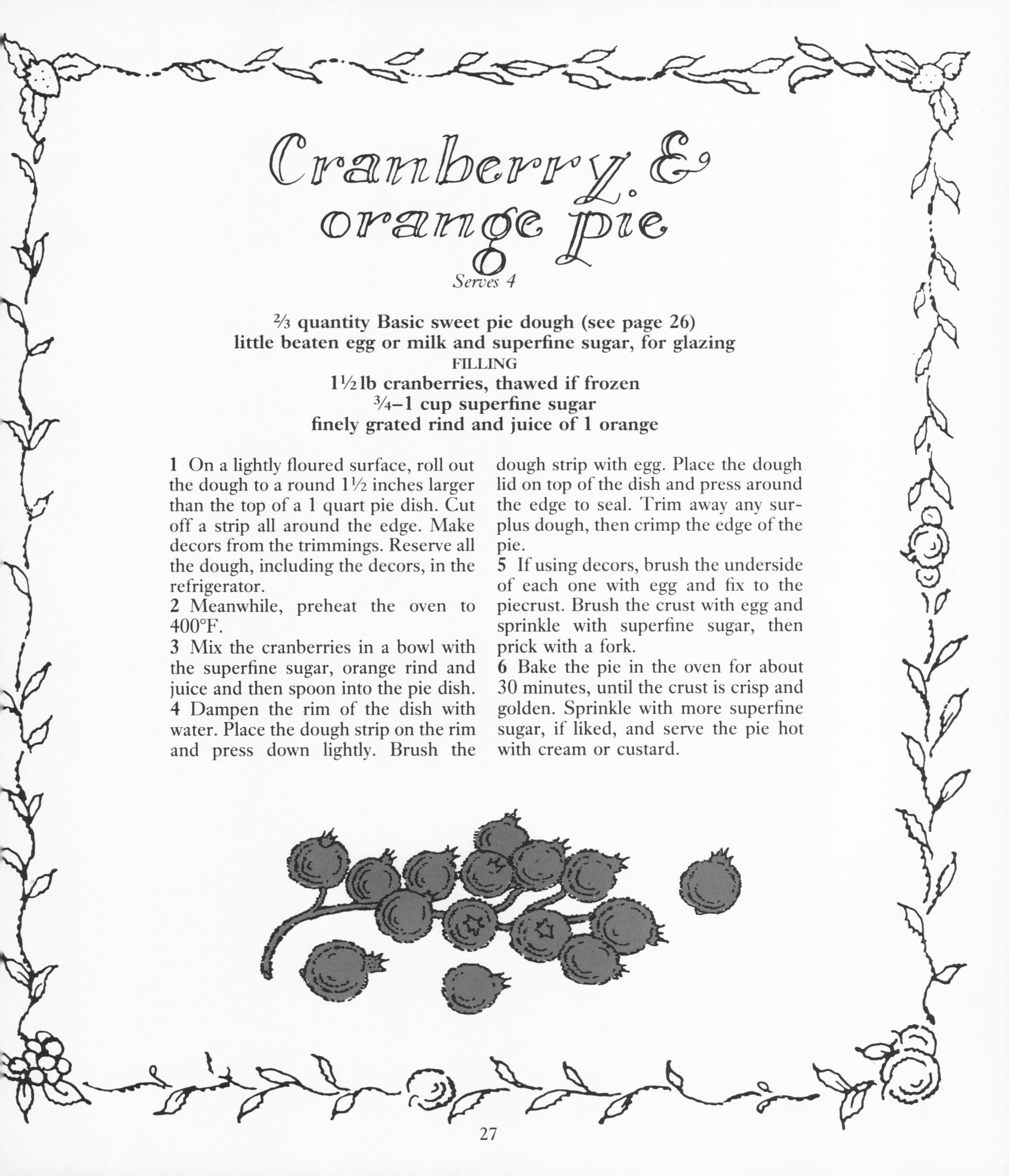

Cranberry & orange pie

Serves 4

⅔ quantity Basic sweet pie dough **(see page 26)**
little beaten egg or milk and superfine sugar, for glazing
FILLING
1½ lb cranberries, thawed if frozen
¾–1 cup superfine sugar
finely grated rind and juice of 1 orange

1 On a lightly floured surface, roll out the dough to a round 1½ inches larger than the top of a 1 quart pie dish. Cut off a strip all around the edge. Make decors from the trimmings. Reserve all the dough, including the decors, in the refrigerator.
2 Meanwhile, preheat the oven to 400°F.
3 Mix the cranberries in a bowl with the superfine sugar, orange rind and juice and then spoon into the pie dish.
4 Dampen the rim of the dish with water. Place the dough strip on the rim and press down lightly. Brush the dough strip with egg. Place the dough lid on top of the dish and press around the edge to seal. Trim away any surplus dough, then crimp the edge of the pie.
5 If using decors, brush the underside of each one with egg and fix to the piecrust. Brush the crust with egg and sprinkle with superfine sugar, then prick with a fork.
6 Bake the pie in the oven for about 30 minutes, until the crust is crisp and golden. Sprinkle with more superfine sugar, if liked, and serve the pie hot with cream or custard.

Rich chestnut pie

Serves 8

⅔ quantity Basic sweet pie dough (see page 26)

FILLING

¾ cup superfine sugar
2 packages (3 oz size) cream cheese
2 eggs, separated
2 cups unsweetened chestnut purée
1 tablespoon all-purpose flour
⅓ cup heavy cream, whipped
2 tablespoons confectioners' sugar

ICING

½ cup confectioners' sugar, sifted
2–3 teaspoons warm water

1 Preheat the oven to 350°F.

2 Roll out the dough on a lightly floured surface and use to line a 10 inch loose-bottomed pie pan. Refrigerate for 15 minutes.

3 Meanwhile, make filling: In a bowl, beat 2 tablespoons of the superfine sugar with the cheese until soft and smooth. Beat in the egg yolks, one at a time, followed by the chestnut purée and then the flour. Stir in ½ cup more of the superfine sugar, or to taste and fold in the whipped cream.

4 In a clean dry bowl, beat the egg whites to stiff peaks, then beat in the confectioners' sugar, 1 tablespoon at a time, until stiff and glossy. Fold the egg whites and the sugar into the chestnut mixture and then transfer to the chilled pie shell.

5 Bake in the oven about 1¼–1½ hours or until the top of the pie is rich golden brown and spongy to the touch in the center.

6 Let cool and carefully remove the pie from the pan and place it on a dish. The top of the pie will sink a little and the surface become firm as it cools.

7 Mix the confectioners' sugar with just enough warm water to give the consistency of heavy cream. Trickle over the pie and serve cold.

Spiced milk pie

Serves 8

1 quantity Basic sweet pie dough (see page 26)
butter, for greasing
5 tablespoons cornstarch
3 tablespoons superfine sugar
3 cups milk
2 tablespoons butter
1 teaspoon grated orange rind
3 eggs, well beaten
1½ teaspoons ground cinnamon

1 Preheat the oven to 375°F. Grease a 10 inch springform pie pan. Roll out the dough on a floured surface and use to line the pan.

2 Line the pie shell with waxed paper and pie weights and bake blind for 10 minutes, then remove the weights and lining paper and bake for 5 minutes more until golden.

3 In a small bowl, mix the cornstarch with a little cold water to a smooth cream.

4 Set aside 2 teaspoons of the superfine sugar. Put the milk, remaining sugar, butter and orange rind in a pan and bring to a boil. Stir some of the hot milk into the cornstarch cream and then stir the cornstarch mixture into the pan. Stir the mixture over very low heat for 5 minutes.

5 Stir in the eggs slowly and cook, stirring continuously, for 3 minutes. Remove the pan from the heat and let cool to a lukewarm temperature.

6 Pour the cooled filling into the pastry shell. Bake for about 20 minutes or until lightly set in the center. Sprinkle with the reserved superfine sugar and the cinnamon and serve the pie hot or cold.

Bakewell tart

Serves 6–8

½ package (17¼ oz size) frozen puff pastry, thawed
FILLING
1 egg
3 egg yolks
⅔ cup superfine sugar
½ cup finely ground almonds
⅔ cup butter
4 tablespoons red jam
custard or cream, to serve

1 Roll out the pastry on a lightly floured surface and use to line a 1 quart shallow pie dish. Prick base well with a fork. Cover and refrigerate.
2 Place the whole egg, egg yolks and sugar in a bowl and beat for about 5 minutes, or until pale and thick and frothy. Stir in the almonds, then cover and refrigerate for at least 30 minutes, or preferably overnight.
3 Preheat the oven to 350°F.
4 Melt the butter in a pan over very low heat, stirring occasionally, then let cool for about 10 minutes. Meanwhile, spread the red jam evenly over the base of the pie shell.
5 Using a wooden spoon beat the egg and almond mixture until smooth, then gradually beat in the cooled butter. Pour into the pie shell and bake in the oven for about 1 hour 20 minutes, covering the pie with a foil tent after 10 minutes to prevent over-browning, until the filling is firm to the touch.
6 Serve warm, with custard or cream.

Grapefruit chiffon pie

Serves 6–8

2 cups shredded coconut
¾ cup butter
½ cup packed light brown sugar
coarsely grated rind of 1 grapefruit
FILLING
1 cup grapefruit juice
1 envelope unflavored gelatin
4 eggs, separated
⅔ cup sugar
¼ teaspoon salt
coarsely grated rind of 1 grapefruit
1 cup heavy cream

1 Make the pie shell: Toast the coconut in a dry skillet, turning constantly with a spatula, until it is lightly browned. Transfer it to a bowl. Melt the butter and pour it over the coconut. Stir in the sugar and grapefruit rind. Use the mixture to line a deep 9 inch pie dish. Chill the pie shell while you make the filling.

2 Put ¼ cup of the grapefruit juice in a small bowl and sprinkle the gelatin over the top. Let soak for 5 minutes or until spongy.

3 Place the remaining grapefruit juice in a pan over a low heat. Stir in the gelatin and remove from the heat as soon as all the gelatin has dissolved.

4 Place the egg yolks and ½ cup sugar in the top part of a double boiler. Beat until smooth, then beat in the gelatin mixture. Continue beating over boiling water for about 10 minutes until the mixture begins to thicken. Stir in the salt and grapefruit rind. Pour into a bowl, let cool, then refrigerate for about 1 hour, or until the mixture begins to set.

5 Beat the egg whites in a large clean dry bowl with the rest of the sugar to soft peaks. Whip the cream in another bowl. Fold the whipped cream and egg whites into the grapefruit mixture.

6 Spoon the mixture into the chilled pie shell and chill for at least 2 hours, or until the filling is firm, before serving the chiffon pie.

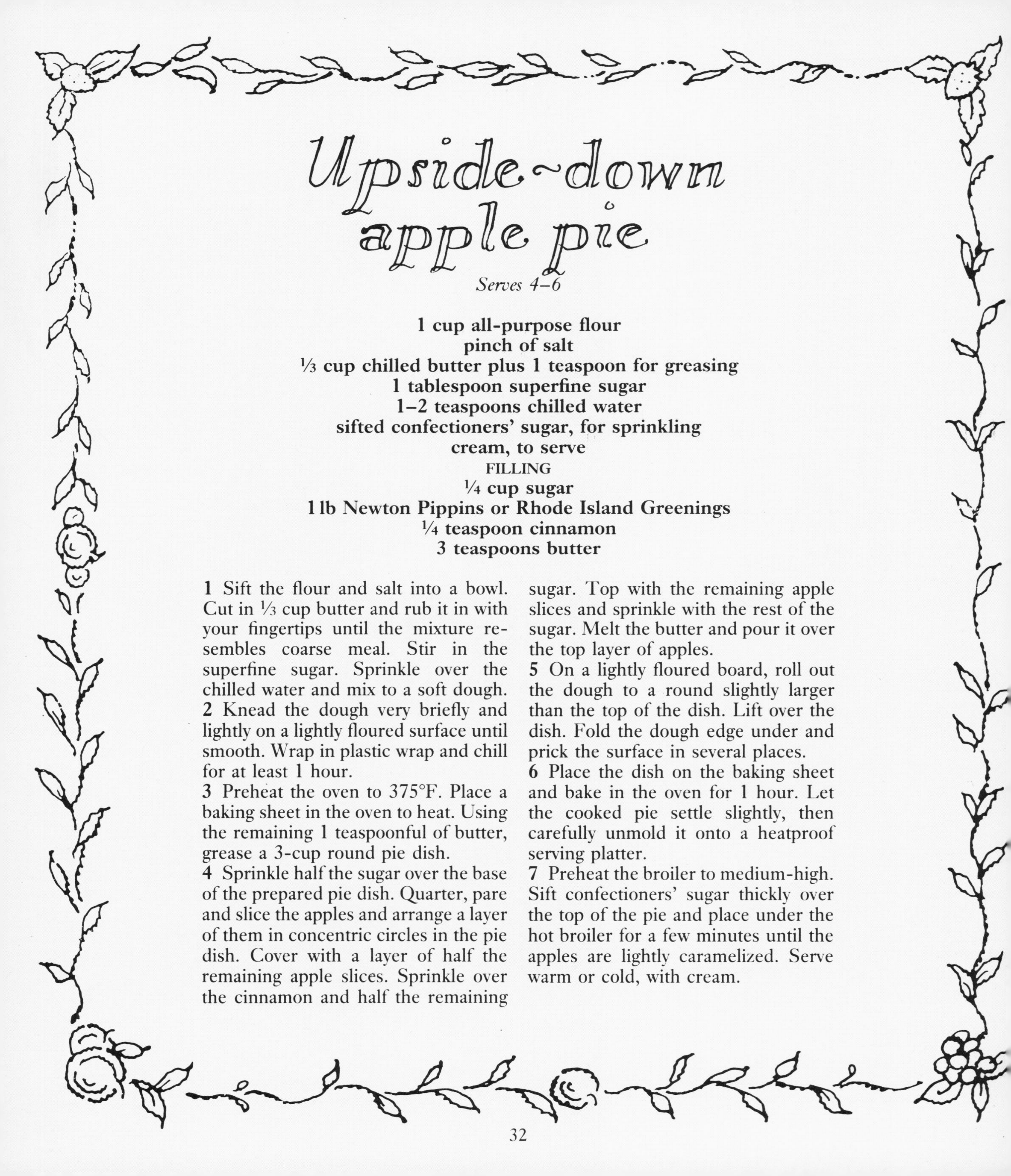

Upside-down apple pie

Serves 4–6

1 cup all-purpose flour
pinch of salt
⅓ cup chilled butter plus 1 teaspoon for greasing
1 tablespoon superfine sugar
1–2 teaspoons chilled water
sifted confectioners' sugar, for sprinkling
cream, to serve

FILLING

¼ cup sugar
1 lb Newton Pippins or Rhode Island Greenings
¼ teaspoon cinnamon
3 teaspoons butter

1 Sift the flour and salt into a bowl. Cut in ⅓ cup butter and rub it in with your fingertips until the mixture resembles coarse meal. Stir in the superfine sugar. Sprinkle over the chilled water and mix to a soft dough.

2 Knead the dough very briefly and lightly on a lightly floured surface until smooth. Wrap in plastic wrap and chill for at least 1 hour.

3 Preheat the oven to 375°F. Place a baking sheet in the oven to heat. Using the remaining 1 teaspoonful of butter, grease a 3-cup round pie dish.

4 Sprinkle half the sugar over the base of the prepared pie dish. Quarter, pare and slice the apples and arrange a layer of them in concentric circles in the pie dish. Cover with a layer of half the remaining apple slices. Sprinkle over the cinnamon and half the remaining sugar. Top with the remaining apple slices and sprinkle with the rest of the sugar. Melt the butter and pour it over the top layer of apples.

5 On a lightly floured board, roll out the dough to a round slightly larger than the top of the dish. Lift over the dish. Fold the dough edge under and prick the surface in several places.

6 Place the dish on the baking sheet and bake in the oven for 1 hour. Let the cooked pie settle slightly, then carefully unmold it onto a heatproof serving platter.

7 Preheat the broiler to medium-high. Sift confectioners' sugar thickly over the top of the pie and place under the hot broiler for a few minutes until the apples are lightly caramelized. Serve warm or cold, with cream.

Spiced fig pie

Serves 6

⅔ quantity Basic sweet pie dough (see page 26)
1 large egg white, lightly beaten
FILLING
1½ cups chopped dried figs
5 tablespoons honey
½ teaspoon ground allspice
1 large egg yolk
1 large egg
4 teaspoons all-purpose flour
1 cup light cream
1 tablespoon slivered almonds

1 Put the figs, honey and allspice for the filling into a bowl. Mix together well, then cover and let stand for about 30 minutes.
2 Meanwhile, preheat the oven to 375°F.
3 On a lightly floured surface, roll out the dough and use to line an 8 inch springform pie pan. Brush with egg white, then prick in several places with a fork. Refrigerate while you finish preparing the spiced fig filling.
4 Add any remaining egg white to the egg yolk and whole egg in a bowl and beat together. Beat in the flour, then gradually beat in the cream. Pour over the fig mixture and stir briskly until well mixed.
5 Spoon the mixture into the pie shell using the tip of a knife to distribute the figs. Sprinkle over the almonds. Bake in the oven for about 40 minutes, or until the filling is puffed, golden and set in the center. Serve warm or cold.

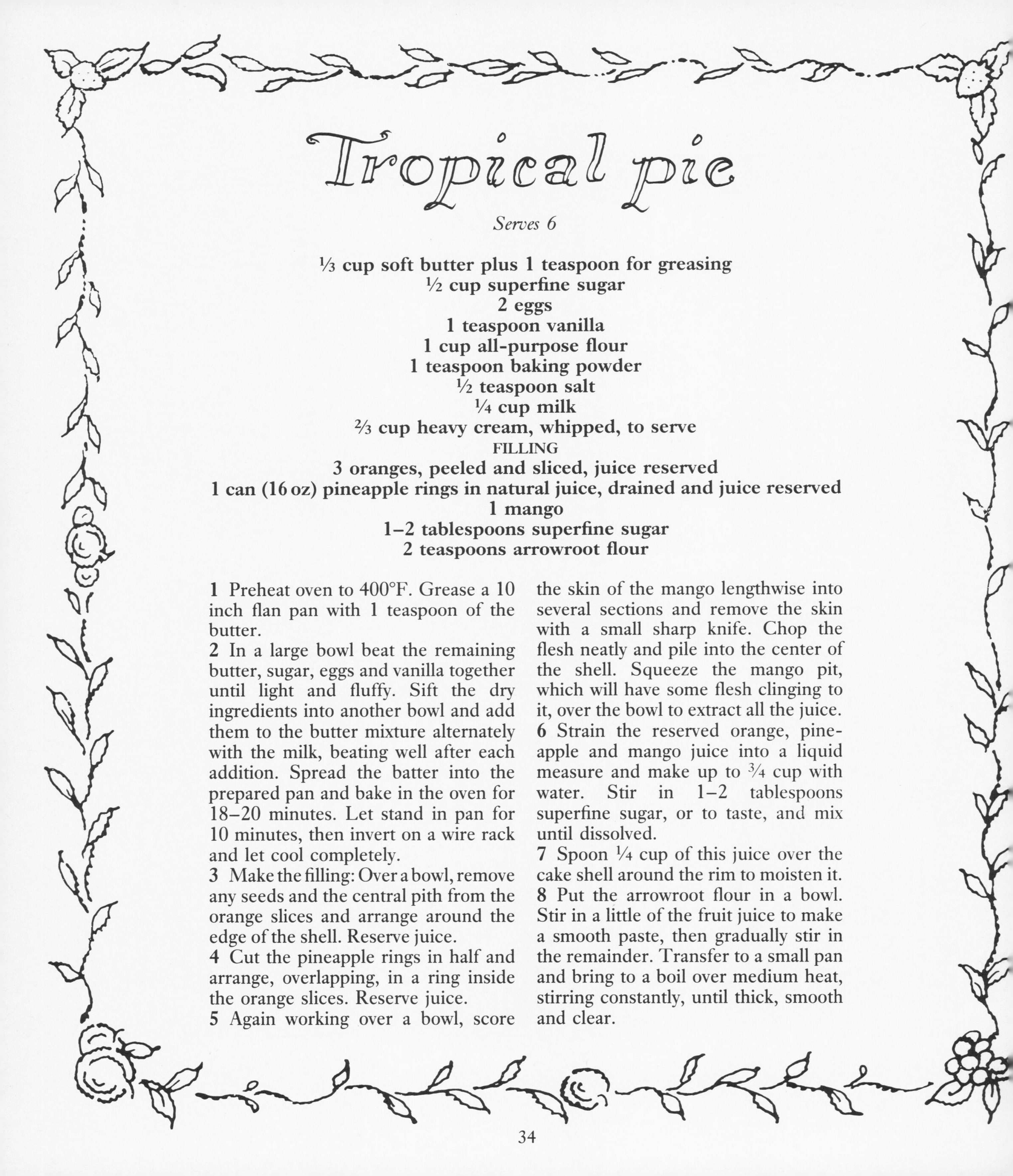

Tropical pie

Serves 6

⅓ cup soft butter plus 1 teaspoon for greasing
½ cup superfine sugar
2 eggs
1 teaspoon vanilla
1 cup all-purpose flour
1 teaspoon baking powder
½ teaspoon salt
¼ cup milk
⅔ cup heavy cream, whipped, to serve

FILLING

3 oranges, peeled and sliced, juice reserved
1 can (16 oz) pineapple rings in natural juice, drained and juice reserved
1 mango
1–2 tablespoons superfine sugar
2 teaspoons arrowroot flour

1 Preheat oven to 400°F. Grease a 10 inch flan pan with 1 teaspoon of the butter.

2 In a large bowl beat the remaining butter, sugar, eggs and vanilla together until light and fluffy. Sift the dry ingredients into another bowl and add them to the butter mixture alternately with the milk, beating well after each addition. Spread the batter into the prepared pan and bake in the oven for 18–20 minutes. Let stand in pan for 10 minutes, then invert on a wire rack and let cool completely.

3 Make the filling: Over a bowl, remove any seeds and the central pith from the orange slices and arrange around the edge of the shell. Reserve juice.

4 Cut the pineapple rings in half and arrange, overlapping, in a ring inside the orange slices. Reserve juice.

5 Again working over a bowl, score the skin of the mango lengthwise into several sections and remove the skin with a small sharp knife. Chop the flesh neatly and pile into the center of the shell. Squeeze the mango pit, which will have some flesh clinging to it, over the bowl to extract all the juice.

6 Strain the reserved orange, pineapple and mango juice into a liquid measure and make up to ¾ cup with water. Stir in 1–2 tablespoons superfine sugar, or to taste, and mix until dissolved.

7 Spoon ¼ cup of this juice over the cake shell around the rim to moisten it.

8 Put the arrowroot flour in a bowl. Stir in a little of the fruit juice to make a smooth paste, then gradually stir in the remainder. Transfer to a small pan and bring to a boil over medium heat, stirring constantly, until thick, smooth and clear.

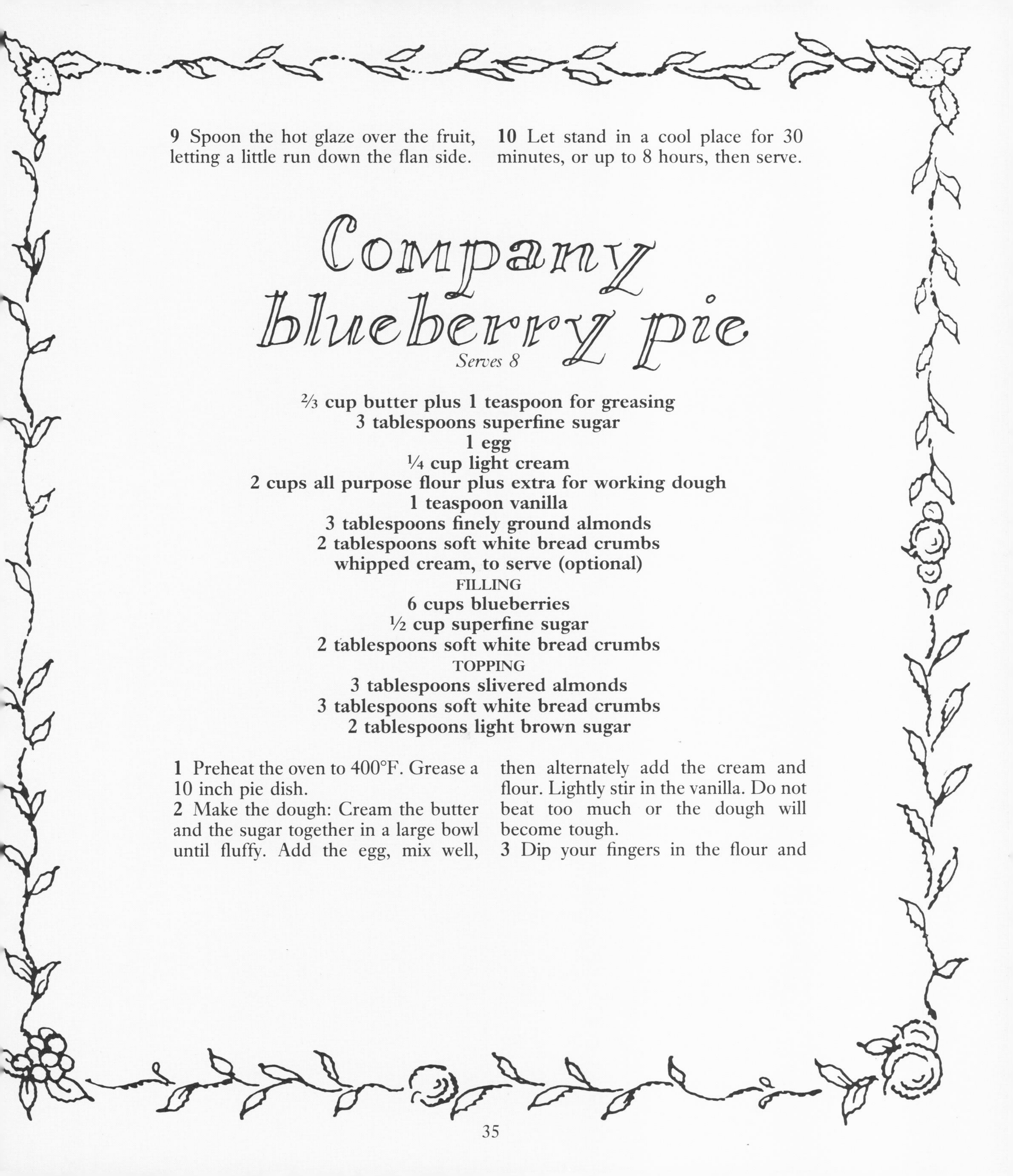

9 Spoon the hot glaze over the fruit, letting a little run down the flan side.

10 Let stand in a cool place for 30 minutes, or up to 8 hours, then serve.

Company blueberry pie

Serves 8

⅔ cup butter plus 1 teaspoon for greasing
3 tablespoons superfine sugar
1 egg
¼ cup light cream
2 cups all purpose flour plus extra for working dough
1 teaspoon vanilla
3 tablespoons finely ground almonds
2 tablespoons soft white bread crumbs
whipped cream, to serve (optional)

FILLING

6 cups blueberries
½ cup superfine sugar
2 tablespoons soft white bread crumbs

TOPPING

3 tablespoons slivered almonds
3 tablespoons soft white bread crumbs
2 tablespoons light brown sugar

1 Preheat the oven to 400°F. Grease a 10 inch pie dish.

2 Make the dough: Cream the butter and the sugar together in a large bowl until fluffy. Add the egg, mix well, then alternately add the cream and flour. Lightly stir in the vanilla. Do not beat too much or the dough will become tough.

3 Dip your fingers in the flour and

spread the dough in the pie dish to make a shell.
4 Scatter the ground almonds and bread crumbs in the shell.
5 Make the filling: In a bowl, mix the blueberries and sugar with the bread crumbs and spread the mixture over the pie shell.
6 Mix the topping ingredients in a small bowl and sprinkle lightly on top of the blueberries.
7 Bake the pie in the oven for about 30 minutes or until the shell is cooked and the almonds in the topping are golden brown. Let the pie cool and serve warm or cold.

Pecan & honey pie

Serves 6

1½ quantity Cream cheese dough (see page 25)
butter, for greasing
FILLING
1¼ cups pecans
⅔ cup honey
¼ cup rum
ICING
1½ cups confectioners' sugar
2 tablespoons water
1 teaspoon lemon juice

1 Grease a 10 inch springform pie pan.
2 Cut off three-quarters of the dough and set it aside. Roll out the remaining dough on a lightly floured board, and use it to line the pie pan. Chill until required, with the remaining dough.
3 Blanch the pecans in boiling water for 15 seconds. Strain and, as soon as the pecans are cool enough to handle, remove as much of the brown skin as possible. Chop the nuts finely or grind them in a food processor, but do not reduce to a paste.
4 Combine the pecans, honey and rum in a bowl and mix thoroughly. Place the filling in the pie shell, pressing it down lightly.
5 Roll out the reserved dough on a floured board to a round large enough to cover the pan. Place the round on top of the pie filling and press the dough edges together to seal. Chill the filled pie for 30 minutes.
6 Preheat the oven to 375°F.
7 Bake the pie for 45–60 minutes or until the crust has shrunk a little and is a golden color. Let cool.
8 Sift the confectioners' sugar into a small an and add the water. Stir over very low heat until a smooth glossy syrup forms that will coat the back of a wooden spoon. Add the lemon juice, stir well and brush over the top of the pie. Allow the icing to set before serving the dessert.

Transparent pie

Serves 4–6

⅔ quantity Basic sweet pie dough (see page 26)
1 cup light corn syrup
1½ cups soft white bread crumbs
grated rind and juice of ½ lemon
whipped cream or custard, to serve (optional)

1 Preheat the oven to 400°F.

2 Roll out the dough thinly on a lightly floured surface and line an 8 inch springform pie pan. Trim the edges and reserve the trimmings. Prick the pie shell with a fork and refrigerate.

3 Make the filling: Put the syrup, bread crumbs, lemon rind and juice in a small pan and heat gently, stirring, until the ingredients are thoroughly mixed. Let cool before spooning into the prepared pie shell.

4 Roll out the reserved dough trimmings and cut in long, ¼ inch-wide strips. Use to decorate the top of the pie in a lattice pattern, moistening the ends of the lattice strips and pressing them firmly against the edge of the pie shell so they do not come loose during baking.

5 Bake in the oven for about 25 minutes or until the lattice is golden and the filling is just set. Serve the pie warm or cold with whipped cream, vanilla ice cream or custard.

Red jam pie

Serves 6–8

⅔ cup soft butter plus extra for greasing
⅔ cup superfine sugar
few drops of vanilla
1 egg, lightly beaten
1 cup finely ground almonds
1½ cups sifted all-purpose flour, sifted
1 lb red jam
confectioners' sugar, for sprinkling
whipped cream, to serve

1 Preheat the oven to 350°F. Butter an 8 inch springform pie pan.
2 Beat the butter and superfine sugar together in a large bowl until very pale and fluffy, then beat in the vanilla. Add the egg, a little at a time, beating thoroughly after each addition. Using a wooden spoon, gradually work in the almonds and flour.
3 Draw the mixture into a ball with your fingers, place on a lightly floured surface and knead briefly until smooth.
4 Reserve one-fourth of the dough in a cool place. With your hand, gently press the remaining dough over the base and 1½ inches of the way up the side of the pan. Neaten the edges.
5 Spread the jam evenly in the pie shell.
6 On a lightly floured surface, roll out the reserved dough to an 8½ × 2 inch strip. Trim edges with a sharp knife, then cut lengthwise in 6 narrow strips.
7 Dampen the ends of the dough strips, then arrange over the jam in a lattice pattern. Press the ends against the shell edge to seal, then flute the rim. Bake in the oven for 45 minutes, or until the lattice is cooked and browned.
8 Sift confectioners' sugar over the top of the hot pie, if liked. Let cool completely, then remove from the pan and transfer to a serving platter.

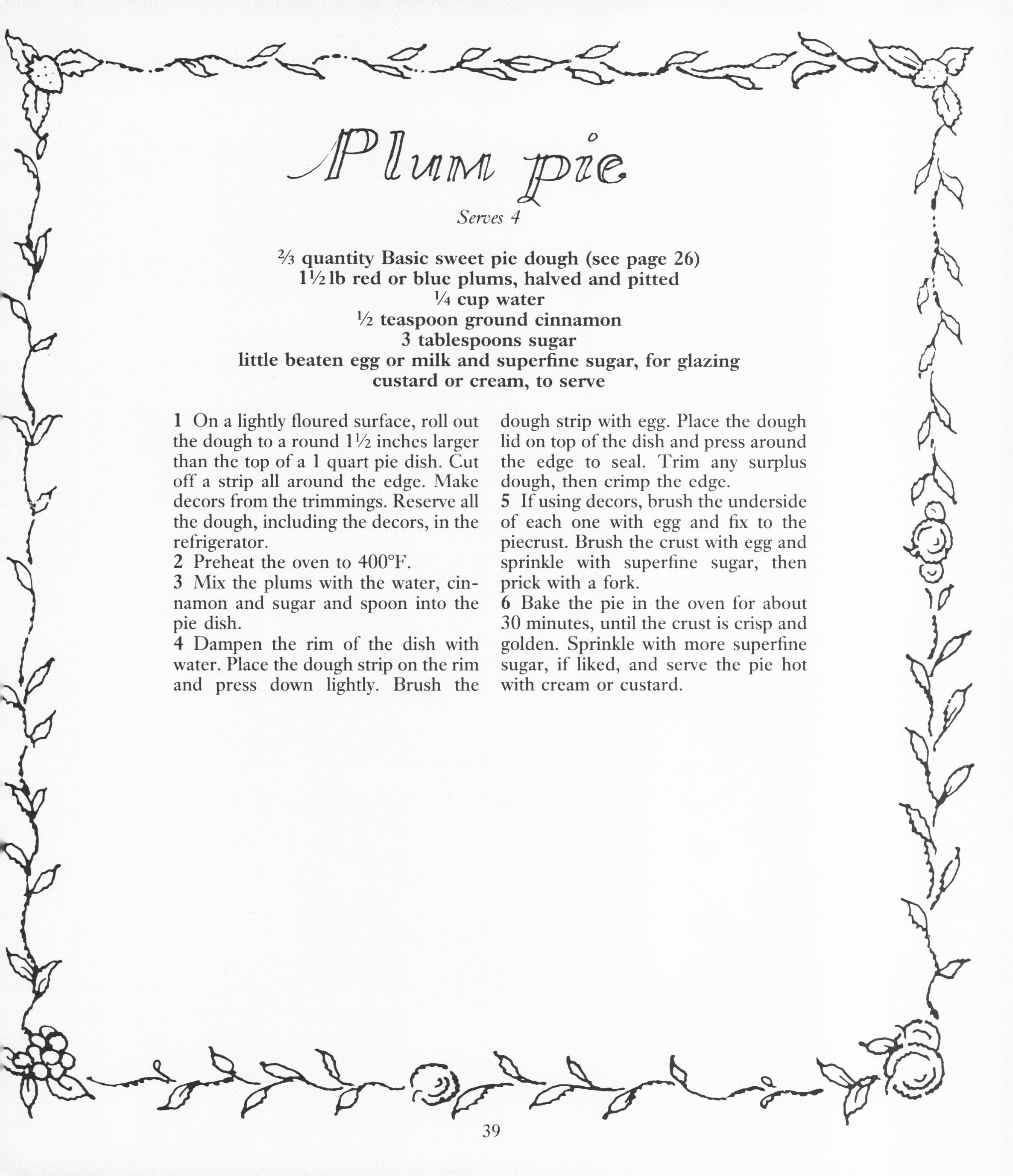

Plum pie

Serves 4

⅔ quantity Basic sweet pie dough (see page 26)
1½ lb red or blue plums, halved and pitted
¼ cup water
½ teaspoon ground cinnamon
3 tablespoons sugar
little beaten egg or milk and superfine sugar, for glazing
custard or cream, to serve

1 On a lightly floured surface, roll out the dough to a round 1½ inches larger than the top of a 1 quart pie dish. Cut off a strip all around the edge. Make decors from the trimmings. Reserve all the dough, including the decors, in the refrigerator.

2 Preheat the oven to 400°F.

3 Mix the plums with the water, cinnamon and sugar and spoon into the pie dish.

4 Dampen the rim of the dish with water. Place the dough strip on the rim and press down lightly. Brush the dough strip with egg. Place the dough lid on top of the dish and press around the edge to seal. Trim any surplus dough, then crimp the edge.

5 If using decors, brush the underside of each one with egg and fix to the piecrust. Brush the crust with egg and sprinkle with superfine sugar, then prick with a fork.

6 Bake the pie in the oven for about 30 minutes, until the crust is crisp and golden. Sprinkle with more superfine sugar, if liked, and serve the pie hot with cream or custard.

Cold Creamy Desserts

These are the desserts with which to impress your guests when you entertain! Among them there are mousses, fools, meringues and rich caramel custards, all of which will add a touch of luxury to the table. These desserts are served chilled so they can be made in advance and either unmolded onto a serving plate or presented in individual dishes or custard cups.

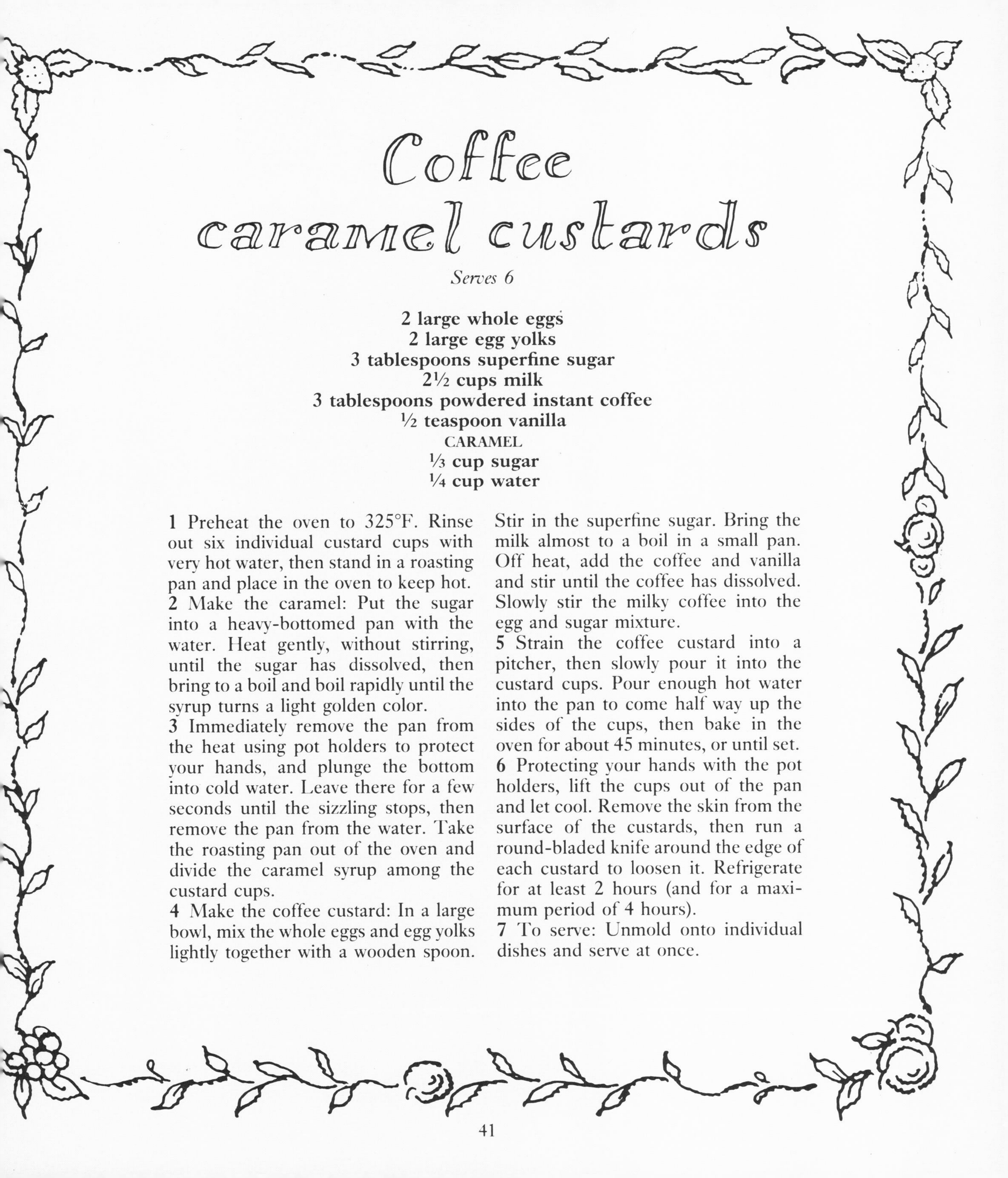

Coffee caramel custards

Serves 6

2 large whole eggs
2 large egg yolks
3 tablespoons superfine sugar
2½ cups milk
3 tablespoons powdered instant coffee
½ teaspoon vanilla
CARAMEL
⅓ cup sugar
¼ cup water

1 Preheat the oven to 325°F. Rinse out six individual custard cups with very hot water, then stand in a roasting pan and place in the oven to keep hot.
2 Make the caramel: Put the sugar into a heavy-bottomed pan with the water. Heat gently, without stirring, until the sugar has dissolved, then bring to a boil and boil rapidly until the syrup turns a light golden color.
3 Immediately remove the pan from the heat using pot holders to protect your hands, and plunge the bottom into cold water. Leave there for a few seconds until the sizzling stops, then remove the pan from the water. Take the roasting pan out of the oven and divide the caramel syrup among the custard cups.
4 Make the coffee custard: In a large bowl, mix the whole eggs and egg yolks lightly together with a wooden spoon. Stir in the superfine sugar. Bring the milk almost to a boil in a small pan. Off heat, add the coffee and vanilla and stir until the coffee has dissolved. Slowly stir the milky coffee into the egg and sugar mixture.
5 Strain the coffee custard into a pitcher, then slowly pour it into the custard cups. Pour enough hot water into the pan to come half way up the sides of the cups, then bake in the oven for about 45 minutes, or until set.
6 Protecting your hands with the pot holders, lift the cups out of the pan and let cool. Remove the skin from the surface of the custards, then run a round-bladed knife around the edge of each custard to loosen it. Refrigerate for at least 2 hours (and for a maximum period of 4 hours).
7 To serve: Unmold onto individual dishes and serve at once.

Old English trifle

Serves 8

2 cups milk
¼ cup superfine sugar
3 eggs
2 egg yolks
½ teaspoon vanilla
8 individual dessert sponge shells or 8 oz yellow cake, cut in thick slices
½ cup raspberry jam
8 small almond macaroons
⅔ cup sweet Madeira wine or sweet sherry
1¼ cups double cream, whipped
¼ cup slivered almonds, toasted
½ cup candied cherries

1 Put the milk in a pan with the sugar and heat gently, stirring until all the sugar has dissolved.
2 In a large heatproof bowl, mix the eggs and egg yolks. Set the bowl over a pan of gently simmering water and, using a rotary beater or hand-held electric mixer, beat until the mixture is thick enough to hold the trail of the beaters for 3–5 seconds when they are lifted.
3 Remove the bowl from the pan, stir in the vanilla and continue to beat until the mixture is cool.
4 Split the sponge shells lengthwise and sandwich them together again with the jam. Arrange them in the bottom of a deep glass dish.
5 Crumble the macaroons over the top and pour over the Madeira or sherry. Let the mixture stand until the liquor is absorbed, then pour over the cold custard. Chill for at least 30 minutes. (The custard will remain slightly soft but should be firm enough to support a decoration.)
6 Pipe rosettes of whipped cream all over the surface, sprinkle with the toasted nuts and arrange the cherries around the edge. Serve at once.

Rum & chocolate cups

Makes 6

9 squares (9 oz) semisweet chocolate, grated
1 tablespoon light rum
½ cup soft butter
½ cup superfine sugar
4 eggs, separated
½ cup finely ground almonds
TO DECORATE
⅔ cup heavy cream, whipped
1 tablespoon finely chopped mixed nuts

1 Put the chocolate in a heatproof bowl with the rum. Set the bowl over a pan half full of simmering water and stir until the chocolate is completely smooth. Let the hot chocolate cool slightly.

2 In a large bowl, beat the butter and sugar together until light and fluffy, then beat in the egg yolks, one at a time. Stir in the chocolate mixture and beat for 5 minutes until creamy. Stir in the ground almonds.

3 In a clean, dry bowl, beat the egg whites to soft peaks, then fold into the chocolate mixture with a metal spoon. Divide among six individual custard cups, level the surfaces and refrigerate for 2 hours until set.

4 To serve: Pipe cream onto the center of each dessert, then sprinkle chopped nuts on top. Serve at once. Italian amaretti cookies or small, bite-size macaroons are a good accompaniment to these rum and chocolate desserts.

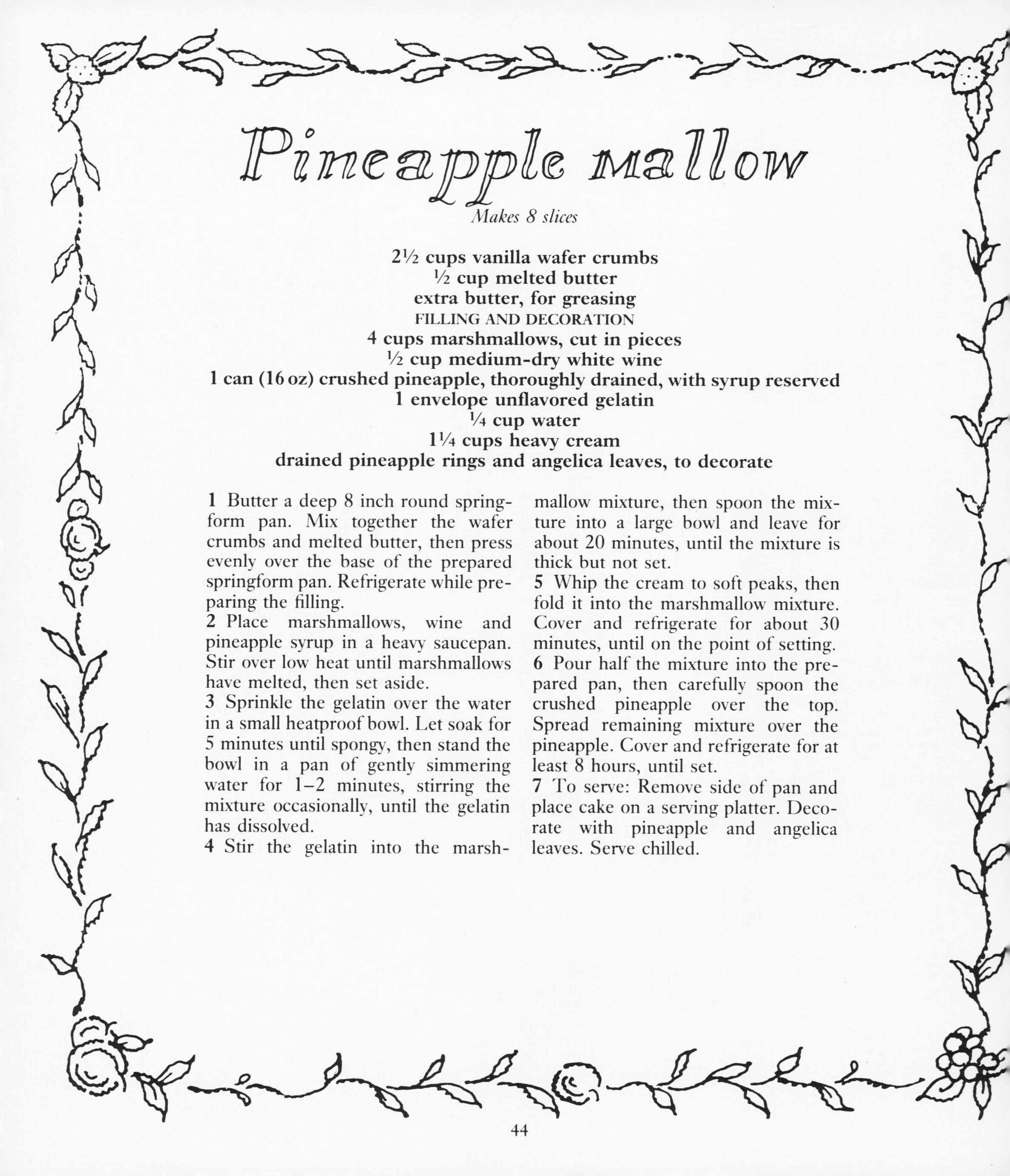

Pineapple mallow

Makes 8 slices

2½ cups vanilla wafer crumbs
½ cup melted butter
extra butter, for greasing
FILLING AND DECORATION
4 cups marshmallows, cut in pieces
½ cup medium-dry white wine
1 can (16 oz) crushed pineapple, thoroughly drained, with syrup reserved
1 envelope unflavored gelatin
¼ cup water
1¼ cups heavy cream
drained pineapple rings and angelica leaves, to decorate

1 Butter a deep 8 inch round springform pan. Mix together the wafer crumbs and melted butter, then press evenly over the base of the prepared springform pan. Refrigerate while preparing the filling.
2 Place marshmallows, wine and pineapple syrup in a heavy saucepan. Stir over low heat until marshmallows have melted, then set aside.
3 Sprinkle the gelatin over the water in a small heatproof bowl. Let soak for 5 minutes until spongy, then stand the bowl in a pan of gently simmering water for 1–2 minutes, stirring the mixture occasionally, until the gelatin has dissolved.
4 Stir the gelatin into the marshmallow mixture, then spoon the mixture into a large bowl and leave for about 20 minutes, until the mixture is thick but not set.
5 Whip the cream to soft peaks, then fold it into the marshmallow mixture. Cover and refrigerate for about 30 minutes, until on the point of setting.
6 Pour half the mixture into the prepared pan, then carefully spoon the crushed pineapple over the top. Spread remaining mixture over the pineapple. Cover and refrigerate for at least 8 hours, until set.
7 To serve: Remove side of pan and place cake on a serving platter. Decorate with pineapple and angelica leaves. Serve chilled.

Chilled blueberry softie

Serves 6

1 can (about 10 oz) blueberries
finely grated rind of 1 orange
1¼ cups heavy cream
1 tablespoon Grand Marnier liqueur
2 egg whites
¼ cup superfine sugar
strips of orange rind, to decorate (optional)
crisp, orange-flavored cookies, to serve

1 Strain the blueberries and their juice into a bowl, or work to a purée in a blender or food processor. Beat in the orange rind then pour into a freezerproof container. Cover and place in the freezer or freezer compartment of the refrigerator until semi-frozen.

2 Whip the cream with the liqueur to soft peaks. In a clean bowl and with clean beaters, beat the egg whites until stiff, then beat in the sugar, 1 tablespoon at a time. Using a large metal spoon, fold the egg whites into the whipped cream.

3 Spoon the semi-frozen purée into a bowl and mash it with a fork, then carefully fold in the cream mixture.

4 Spoon into chilled glasses and decorate with strips of orange rind, if liked. Top each portion with 2 cookies and serve at once.

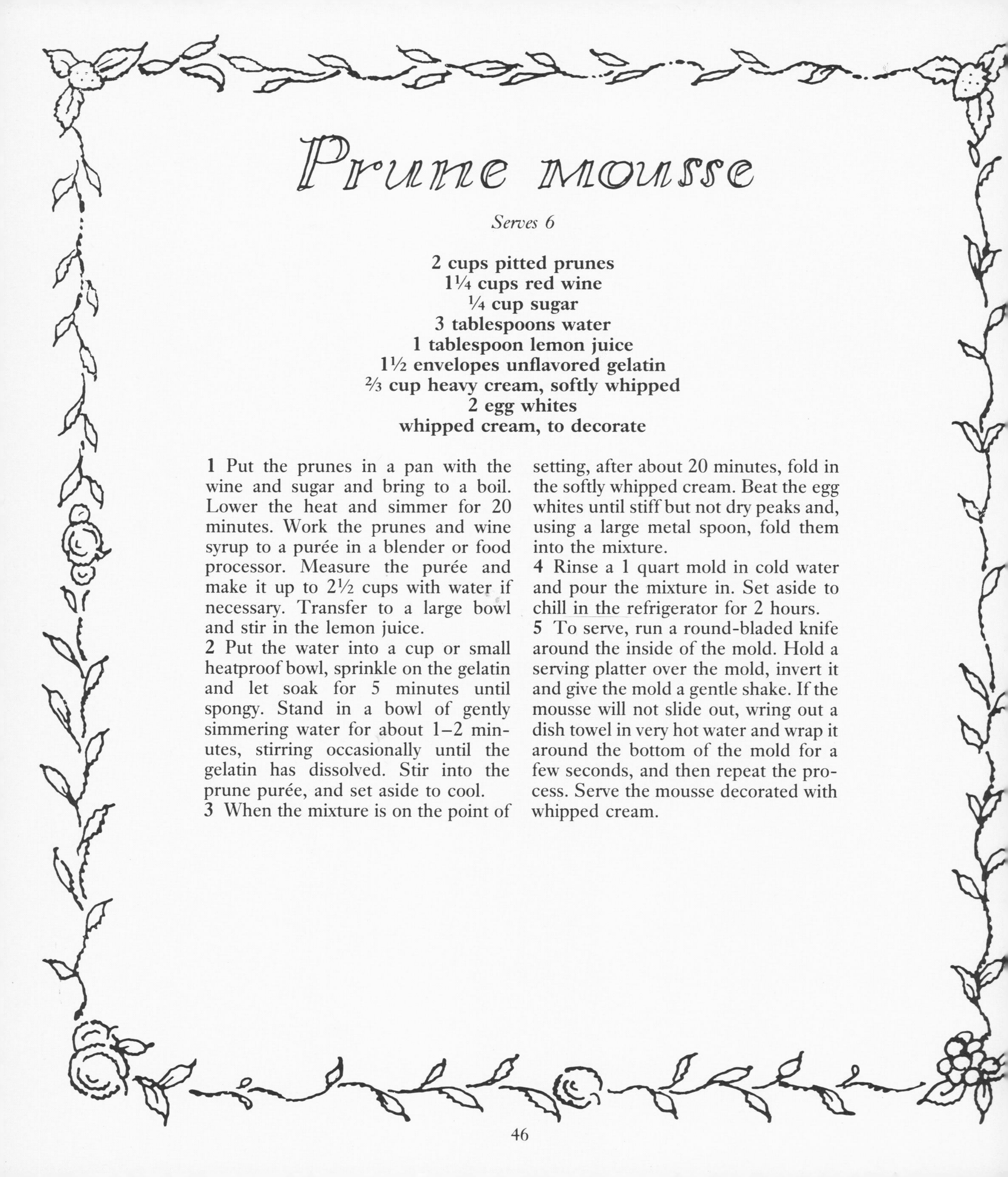

Prune mousse

Serves 6

2 cups pitted prunes
1¼ cups red wine
¼ cup sugar
3 tablespoons water
1 tablespoon lemon juice
1½ envelopes unflavored gelatin
⅔ cup heavy cream, softly whipped
2 egg whites
whipped cream, to decorate

1 Put the prunes in a pan with the wine and sugar and bring to a boil. Lower the heat and simmer for 20 minutes. Work the prunes and wine syrup to a purée in a blender or food processor. Measure the purée and make it up to 2½ cups with water if necessary. Transfer to a large bowl and stir in the lemon juice.
2 Put the water into a cup or small heatproof bowl, sprinkle on the gelatin and let soak for 5 minutes until spongy. Stand in a bowl of gently simmering water for about 1–2 minutes, stirring occasionally until the gelatin has dissolved. Stir into the prune purée, and set aside to cool.
3 When the mixture is on the point of setting, after about 20 minutes, fold in the softly whipped cream. Beat the egg whites until stiff but not dry peaks and, using a large metal spoon, fold them into the mixture.
4 Rinse a 1 quart mold in cold water and pour the mixture in. Set aside to chill in the refrigerator for 2 hours.
5 To serve, run a round-bladed knife around the inside of the mold. Hold a serving platter over the mold, invert it and give the mold a gentle shake. If the mousse will not slide out, wring out a dish towel in very hot water and wrap it around the bottom of the mold for a few seconds, and then repeat the process. Serve the mousse decorated with whipped cream.

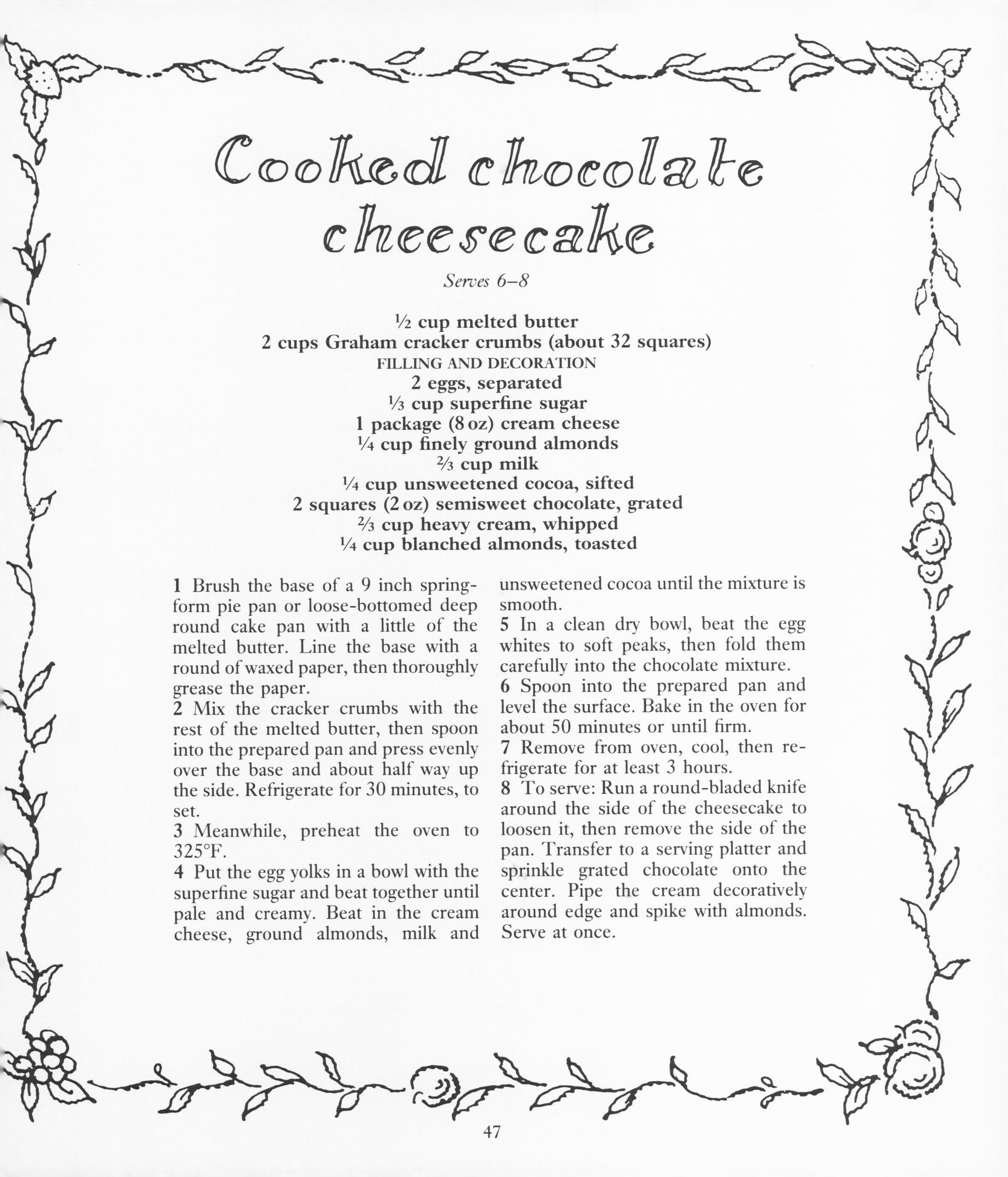

Cooked chocolate cheesecake

Serves 6–8

½ cup melted butter
2 cups Graham cracker crumbs (about 32 squares)
FILLING AND DECORATION
2 eggs, separated
⅓ cup superfine sugar
1 package (8 oz) cream cheese
¼ cup finely ground almonds
⅔ cup milk
¼ cup unsweetened cocoa, sifted
2 squares (2 oz) semisweet chocolate, grated
⅔ cup heavy cream, whipped
¼ cup blanched almonds, toasted

1 Brush the base of a 9 inch spring-form pie pan or loose-bottomed deep round cake pan with a little of the melted butter. Line the base with a round of waxed paper, then thoroughly grease the paper.

2 Mix the cracker crumbs with the rest of the melted butter, then spoon into the prepared pan and press evenly over the base and about half way up the side. Refrigerate for 30 minutes, to set.

3 Meanwhile, preheat the oven to 325°F.

4 Put the egg yolks in a bowl with the superfine sugar and beat together until pale and creamy. Beat in the cream cheese, ground almonds, milk and unsweetened cocoa until the mixture is smooth.

5 In a clean dry bowl, beat the egg whites to soft peaks, then fold them carefully into the chocolate mixture.

6 Spoon into the prepared pan and level the surface. Bake in the oven for about 50 minutes or until firm.

7 Remove from oven, cool, then refrigerate for at least 3 hours.

8 To serve: Run a round-bladed knife around the side of the cheesecake to loosen it, then remove the side of the pan. Transfer to a serving platter and sprinkle grated chocolate onto the center. Pipe the cream decoratively around edge and spike with almonds. Serve at once.

Floating islands

Serves 6

1 quart milk
thinly peeled rind of 1 orange
4 egg whites
1¼ cups superfine sugar
3 tablespoons orange-flavored liqueur or orange juice
1¼ cups light cream
8 egg yolks
vegetable oil, for greasing

CARAMEL

⅓ cup sugar
grated rind and juice of 1 orange
1 tablespoon water

1 Put the milk and orange rind in a wide, shallow saucepan, or a deep skillet with a lid. Heat gently until the milk comes almost to the boiling point, remove from the heat, cover and let stand for 30 minutes.

2 In a spotlessly clean dry bowl, beat the egg whites to stiff peaks. Gradually beat in 1 cup of the superfine sugar, adding 1 tablespoon at a time and beating well between each addition until the egg whites are very stiff.

3 Remove the orange rind from the milk with a slotted spoon, and stir in 1 tablespoon of the liqueur or juice. Place the pan over moderate heat until the milk barely begins to simmer.

4 Drop 6 heaped tablespoons of the beaten egg whites into the simmering milk and cook very gently for 4–5 minutes, until the meringues are set.

5 Carefully lift out the cooked meringues from the milk with a slotted spoon and place on kitchen paper towels to drain, turning them over after a few minutes to drain the other side. Continue cooking the remaining meringue in batches, until about 20 are made, removing any skin from the milk as it forms.

6 Carefully pile the meringue "eggs" in the center of a large serving bowl and set aside.

7 Strain the milk left in the pan into a liquid measure – there should be about 2 cups. Stir the light cream and remaining liqueur or juice into the milk.

8 In a bowl, beat the egg yolks with the remaining superfine sugar until they are light and creamy, then stir in the milk mixture.

9 Strain the egg and milk mixture into a heavy-bottomed saucepan. Cook over very low heat, stirring constantly with a wooden spoon, until the custard is thick enough to thinly coat the back of the spoon and has the consistency of light cream. Immediately strain the custard into a bowl and cover the

surface closely with plastic wrap to prevent a skin forming. Set aside to cool.
10 Brush a baking sheet very lightly with oil. Make the caramel: Put the sugar in a small pan with the orange rind, juice and water. Stir over a low heat until the sugar has completely dissolved, then bring to a boil, without stirring, and boil until the syrup is a dark golden color. Pour the syrup immediately onto the baking sheet and let stand until the caramel is quite cold.
11 Meanwhile, stir the cooled custard, then pour it very carefully round, not over, the meringues in the serving dish. As the custard is poured into the dish the meringues will rise and float on the surface of the custard. Refrigerate for 1–2 hours until cold.
12 Just before serving, put the caramel into a strong plastic bag and crush finely with a rolling pin. Sprinkle over the meringues and serve immediately.

Sweet syllabub

Serves 4

thinly pared rind and juice of ½ orange
¼ cup sweet sherry
¼ cup superfine sugar
pinch of ground cinnamon
2–3 drops almond extract
1¼ cups heavy whipping cream
toasted slivered almonds, to decorate (optional)
brandy roll-ups, to serve

1 Put the orange rind and juice, sherry, superfine sugar, cinnamon and almond extract in a large bowl. Cover and let stand for 2–3 hours.
2 Uncover bowl and remove orange rind. Using a wire whip or a hand-held electric mixer, beat until the superfine sugar has dissolved. Add the cream and continue beating until the mixture is light and fluffy and holds soft peaks when the beater is lifted out of the sugar and cream mixture.
3 Cover and refrigerate for at least 30 minutes and up to 4 hours.
4 To serve: Divide the syllabub equally among 4 chilled dessert glasses. Decorate with nuts, if liked, and serve at once, with roll-ups.

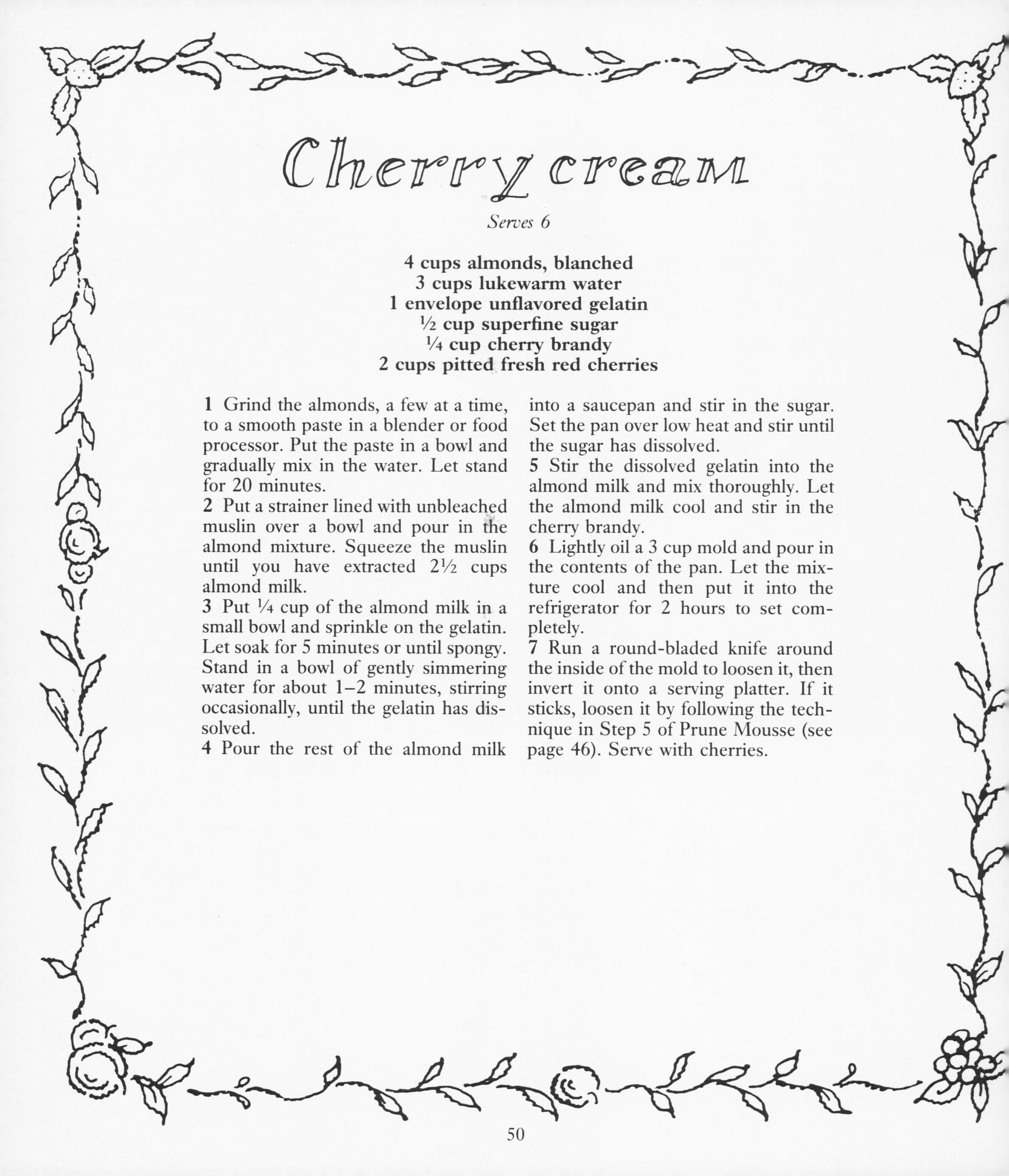

Cherry cream

Serves 6

4 cups almonds, blanched
3 cups lukewarm water
1 envelope unflavored gelatin
½ cup superfine sugar
¼ cup cherry brandy
2 cups pitted fresh red cherries

1 Grind the almonds, a few at a time, to a smooth paste in a blender or food processor. Put the paste in a bowl and gradually mix in the water. Let stand for 20 minutes.

2 Put a strainer lined with unbleached muslin over a bowl and pour in the almond mixture. Squeeze the muslin until you have extracted 2½ cups almond milk.

3 Put ¼ cup of the almond milk in a small bowl and sprinkle on the gelatin. Let soak for 5 minutes or until spongy. Stand in a bowl of gently simmering water for about 1–2 minutes, stirring occasionally, until the gelatin has dissolved.

4 Pour the rest of the almond milk into a saucepan and stir in the sugar. Set the pan over low heat and stir until the sugar has dissolved.

5 Stir the dissolved gelatin into the almond milk and mix thoroughly. Let the almond milk cool and stir in the cherry brandy.

6 Lightly oil a 3 cup mold and pour in the contents of the pan. Let the mixture cool and then put it into the refrigerator for 2 hours to set completely.

7 Run a round-bladed knife around the inside of the mold to loosen it, then invert it onto a serving platter. If it sticks, loosen it by following the technique in Step 5 of Prune Mousse (see page 46). Serve with cherries.

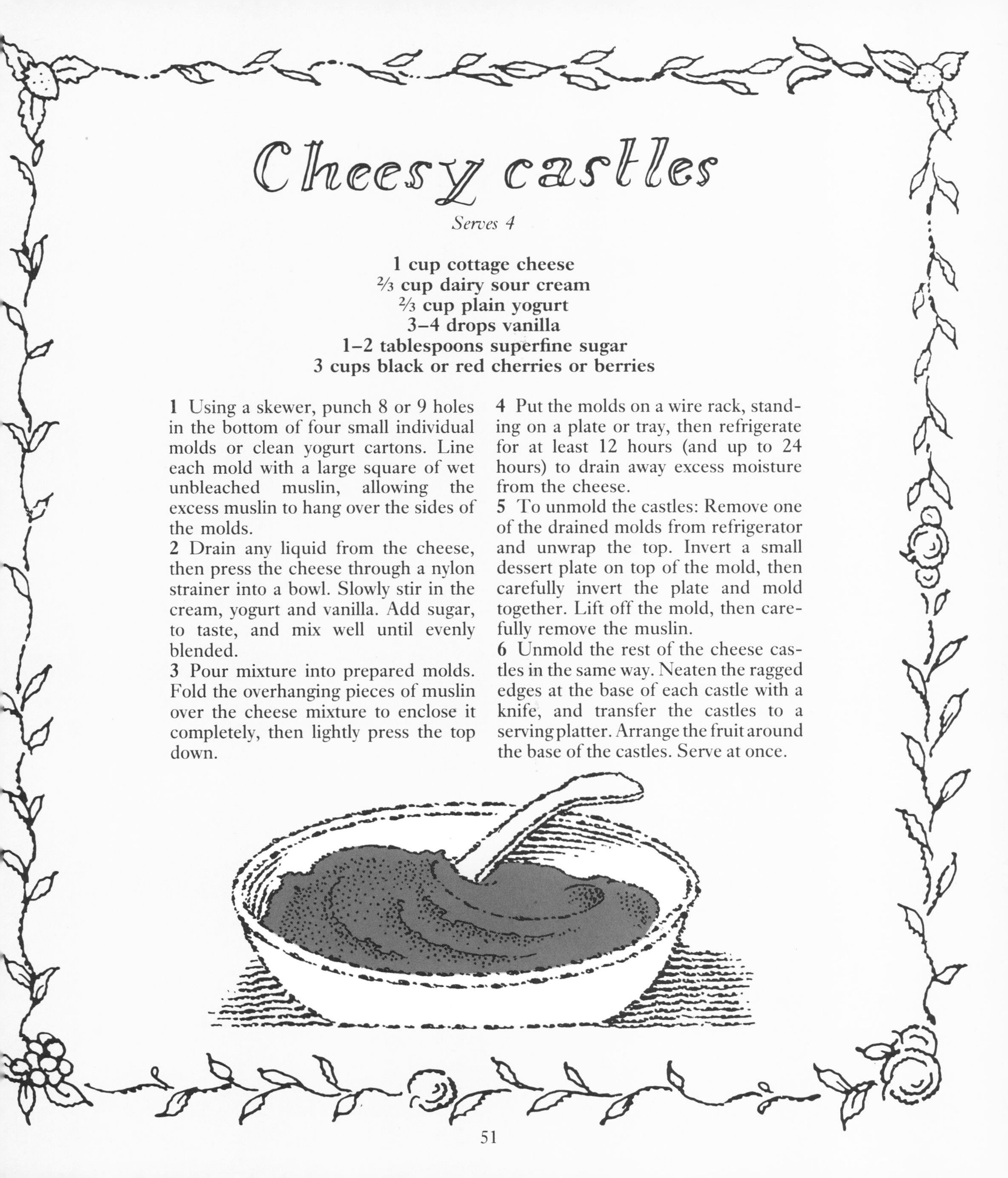

Cheesy castles

Serves 4

1 cup cottage cheese
⅔ cup dairy sour cream
⅔ cup plain yogurt
3–4 drops vanilla
1–2 tablespoons superfine sugar
3 cups black or red cherries or berries

1 Using a skewer, punch 8 or 9 holes in the bottom of four small individual molds or clean yogurt cartons. Line each mold with a large square of wet unbleached muslin, allowing the excess muslin to hang over the sides of the molds.

2 Drain any liquid from the cheese, then press the cheese through a nylon strainer into a bowl. Slowly stir in the cream, yogurt and vanilla. Add sugar, to taste, and mix well until evenly blended.

3 Pour mixture into prepared molds. Fold the overhanging pieces of muslin over the cheese mixture to enclose it completely, then lightly press the top down.

4 Put the molds on a wire rack, standing on a plate or tray, then refrigerate for at least 12 hours (and up to 24 hours) to drain away excess moisture from the cheese.

5 To unmold the castles: Remove one of the drained molds from refrigerator and unwrap the top. Invert a small dessert plate on top of the mold, then carefully invert the plate and mold together. Lift off the mold, then carefully remove the muslin.

6 Unmold the rest of the cheese castles in the same way. Neaten the ragged edges at the base of each castle with a knife, and transfer the castles to a serving platter. Arrange the fruit around the base of the castles. Serve at once.

Chestnut charlotte

Serves 4–5

15–18 slices stale French bread, without crusts
or about ½ lb slab cake, sliced
¾ cup dark rum
1 can (10 oz) whole chestnuts
2 tablespoons superfine sugar
few drops of vanilla
1 tablespoon soft butter
⅔ cup heavy cream, whipped
2 squares (2 oz) semisweet chocolate, grated

1 In a large shallow dish, soak the bread slices in the rum and line a charlotte mold or 1 quart pudding mold with them, reserving enough for sealing the top.

2 Half-drain the chestnuts and work them to a purée in a blender or food processor, adding the rest of the liquid from the can, the superfine sugar, drops of vanilla and the soft butter.

3 Spoon this purée into the mold. Arrange the remaining bread slices on top. Cover with a flat plate that fits inside the mold, weight it down then leave the charlotte in the refrigerator overnight to set.

4 When required, unmold the charlotte onto a platter, cover it with whipped cream and sprinkle generously with grated chocolate.

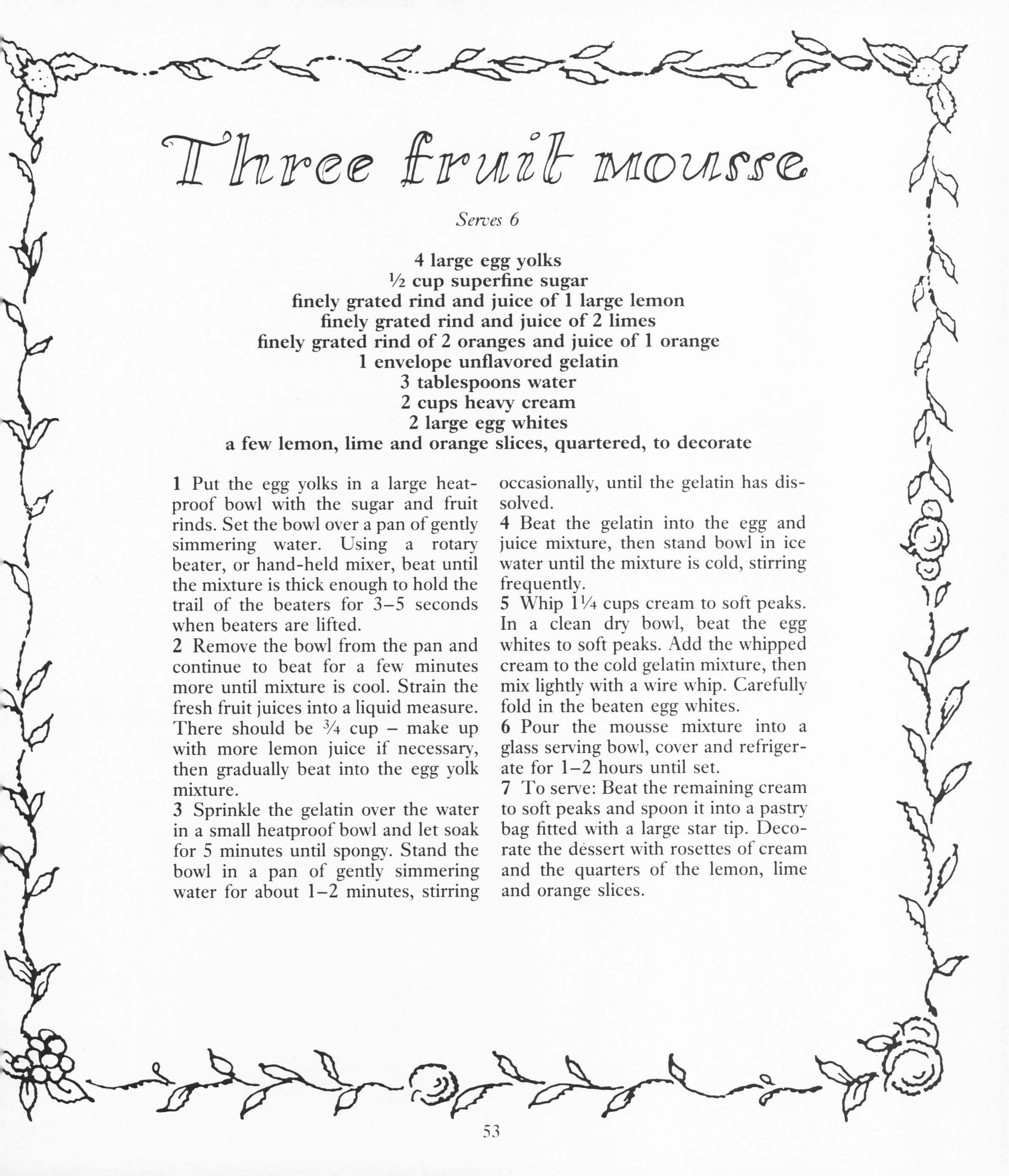

Three fruit mousse

Serves 6

4 large egg yolks
½ cup superfine sugar
finely grated rind and juice of 1 large lemon
finely grated rind and juice of 2 limes
finely grated rind of 2 oranges and juice of 1 orange
1 envelope unflavored gelatin
3 tablespoons water
2 cups heavy cream
2 large egg whites
a few lemon, lime and orange slices, quartered, to decorate

1 Put the egg yolks in a large heatproof bowl with the sugar and fruit rinds. Set the bowl over a pan of gently simmering water. Using a rotary beater, or hand-held mixer, beat until the mixture is thick enough to hold the trail of the beaters for 3–5 seconds when beaters are lifted.

2 Remove the bowl from the pan and continue to beat for a few minutes more until mixture is cool. Strain the fresh fruit juices into a liquid measure. There should be ¾ cup – make up with more lemon juice if necessary, then gradually beat into the egg yolk mixture.

3 Sprinkle the gelatin over the water in a small heatproof bowl and let soak for 5 minutes until spongy. Stand the bowl in a pan of gently simmering water for about 1–2 minutes, stirring occasionally, until the gelatin has dissolved.

4 Beat the gelatin into the egg and juice mixture, then stand bowl in ice water until the mixture is cold, stirring frequently.

5 Whip 1¼ cups cream to soft peaks. In a clean dry bowl, beat the egg whites to soft peaks. Add the whipped cream to the cold gelatin mixture, then mix lightly with a wire whip. Carefully fold in the beaten egg whites.

6 Pour the mousse mixture into a glass serving bowl, cover and refrigerate for 1–2 hours until set.

7 To serve: Beat the remaining cream to soft peaks and spoon it into a pastry bag fitted with a large star tip. Decorate the dessert with rosettes of cream and the quarters of the lemon, lime and orange slices.

Ways With Fruit

Fruit forms the basis of many desserts and is the ideal way to round off a meal. In this chapter there is a wide selection of fruit desserts, some of which are perfect for a family supper while others are more sophisticated – ideal for entertaining. We suggest ways of serving fruit that might not have occurred to you before – who would have thought of poaching pears and serving them with a delicious butterscotch sauce? For parties, the strawberry and almond gateau will add a touch of style to a buffet table, while the orange ice cream cups will refresh jaded taste buds. These desserts are sure to be a success!

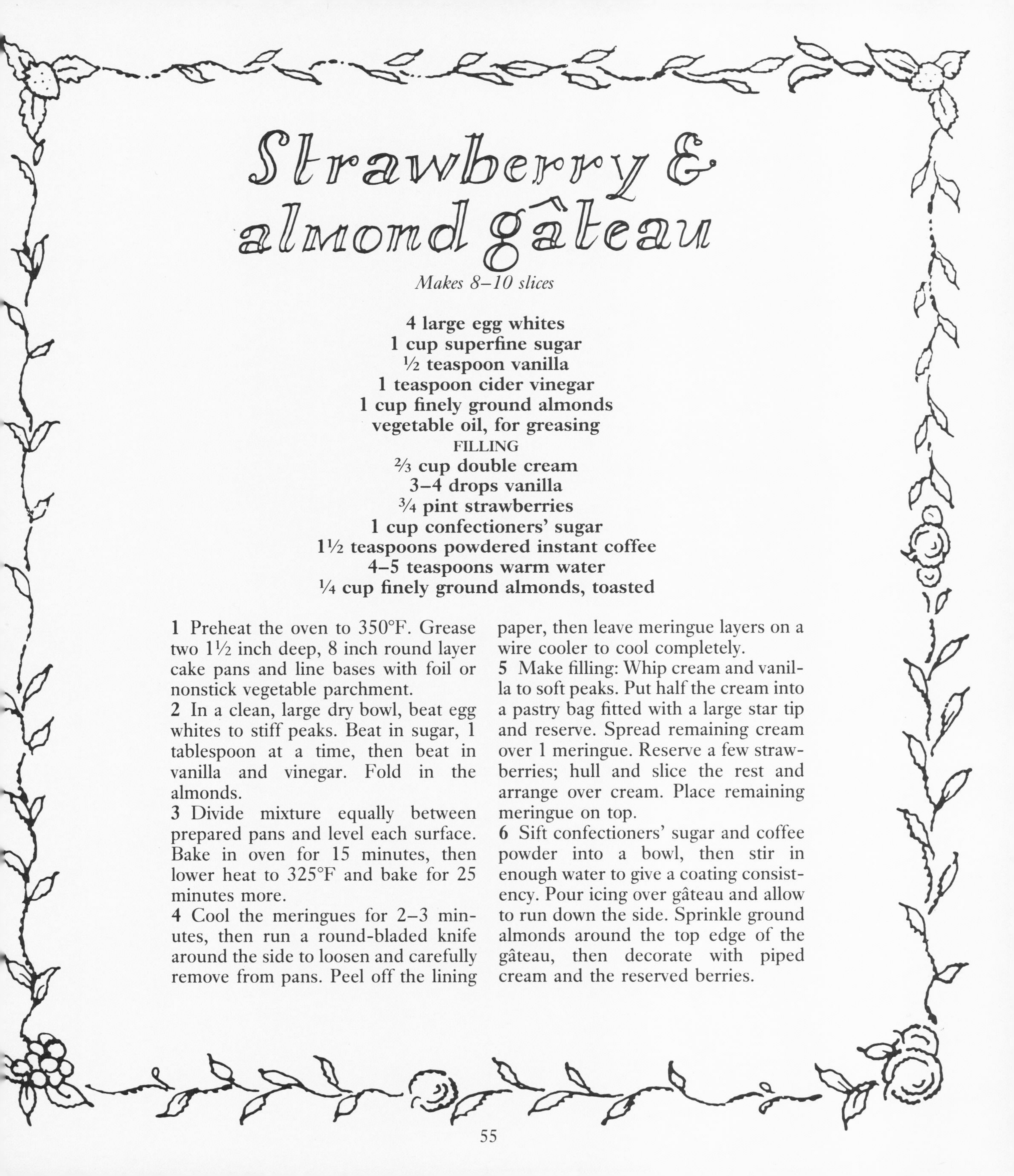

Strawberry & almond gâteau

Makes 8–10 slices

4 large egg whites
1 cup superfine sugar
½ teaspoon vanilla
1 teaspoon cider vinegar
1 cup finely ground almonds
vegetable oil, for greasing
FILLING
⅔ cup double cream
3–4 drops vanilla
¾ pint strawberries
1 cup confectioners' sugar
1½ teaspoons powdered instant coffee
4–5 teaspoons warm water
¼ cup finely ground almonds, toasted

1 Preheat the oven to 350°F. Grease two 1½ inch deep, 8 inch round layer cake pans and line bases with foil or nonstick vegetable parchment.
2 In a clean, large dry bowl, beat egg whites to stiff peaks. Beat in sugar, 1 tablespoon at a time, then beat in vanilla and vinegar. Fold in the almonds.
3 Divide mixture equally between prepared pans and level each surface. Bake in oven for 15 minutes, then lower heat to 325°F and bake for 25 minutes more.
4 Cool the meringues for 2–3 minutes, then run a round-bladed knife around the side to loosen and carefully remove from pans. Peel off the lining paper, then leave meringue layers on a wire cooler to cool completely.
5 Make filling: Whip cream and vanilla to soft peaks. Put half the cream into a pastry bag fitted with a large star tip and reserve. Spread remaining cream over 1 meringue. Reserve a few strawberries; hull and slice the rest and arrange over cream. Place remaining meringue on top.
6 Sift confectioners' sugar and coffee powder into a bowl, then stir in enough water to give a coating consistency. Pour icing over gâteau and allow to run down the side. Sprinkle ground almonds around the top edge of the gâteau, then decorate with piped cream and the reserved berries.

Apricot crêpes

Serves 4

3 tablespoons all-purpose flour
3 tablespoons Graham flour
¼ teaspoon salt
2 eggs
2 tablespoons melted butter
⅔ cup milk
2 tablespoons water
oil, for greasing

FILLING

1 cup dried apricots
⅓ cup packed light brown sugar
3 tablespoons water
1 large tart apple, pared, cored and chopped
1 tablespoon butter

TO FINISH

butter, for greasing
juice of 1 orange
2 tablespoons confectioners' sugar

1 Make the crêpes: Place the flours and salt in a bowl. Beat the eggs and stir into the flour with the melted butter. Stir gently until smooth.

2 Gradually add the milk and water, beating well. Strain the batter, if necessary, to remove any lumps.

3 Heat a 6–7 inch skillet and grease with oil.

4 Spoon 3 tablespoons of the batter into the pan, tilting the pan so that the batter thinly coats the surface. Cook over medium heat for 1 minute until lightly golden underneath.

5 Raise the pan at the handle and turn the crêpe with a spatula. Continue cooking the other side for 1 minute until lightly golden.

6 Stack the crêpes between pieces of waxed paper to prevent them sticking together. Repeat until all the batter is used up greasing the pan between each crêpe. Preheat the oven to 350°F.

7 Place the apricots, sugar, water, apple and butter in a pan and bring to a boil. Cover, lower the heat and simmer gently for 15 minutes.

8 Work the mixture to a purée in a blender or food processor. Lay the crêpes flat on a board and spread the apricot mixture evenly over them. Fold the crêpes to form triangular shapes.

9 Arrange the crêpes, slightly overlapping, in a lightly greased shallow ovenproof dish. Sprinkle with the orange juice and confectioners' sugar.

10 Bake for 15–20 minutes and serve hot with cream, if wished.

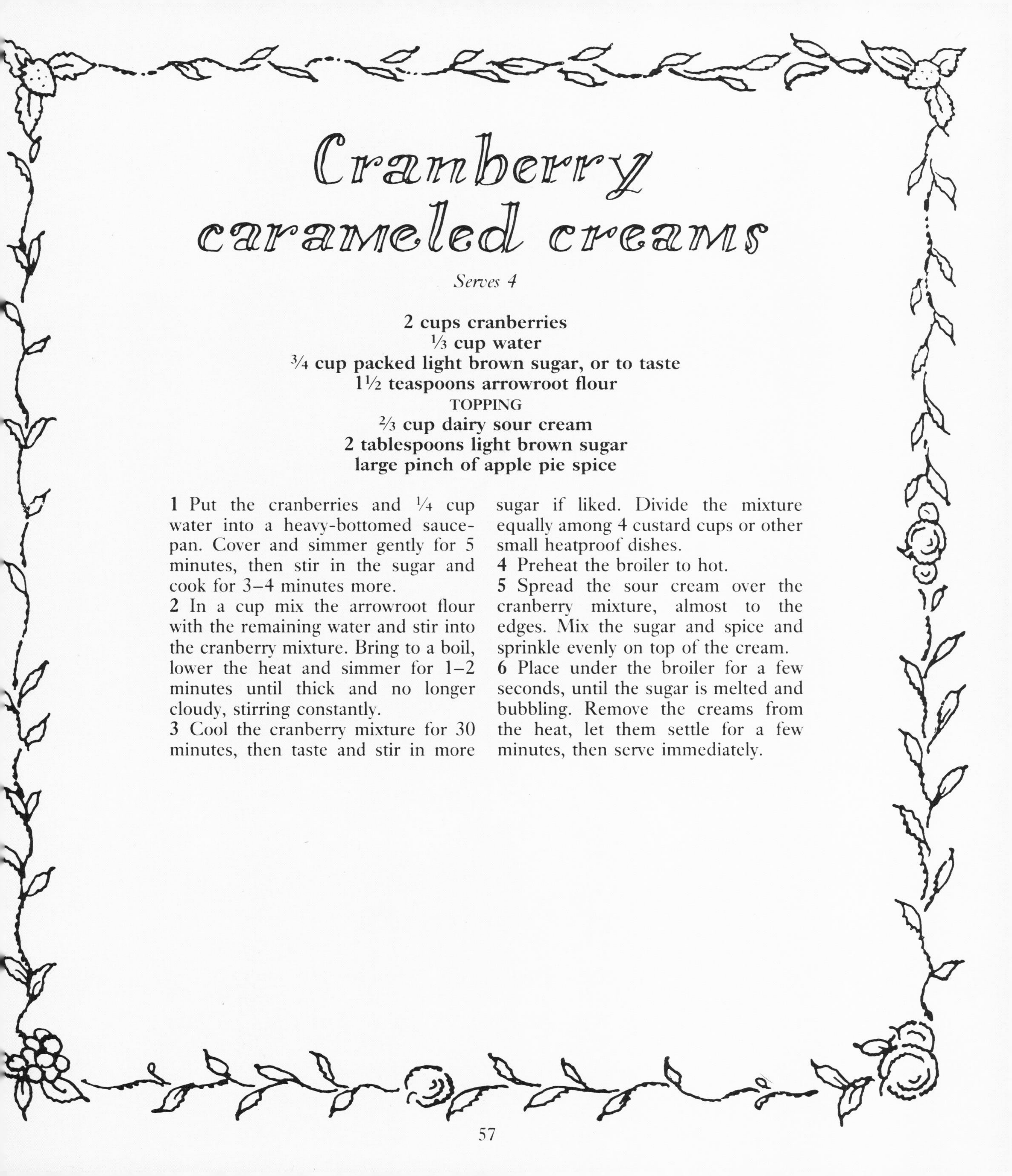

Cranberry carameled creams

Serves 4

2 cups cranberries
⅓ cup water
¾ cup packed light brown sugar, or to taste
1½ teaspoons arrowroot flour

TOPPING

⅔ cup dairy sour cream
2 tablespoons light brown sugar
large pinch of apple pie spice

1 Put the cranberries and ¼ cup water into a heavy-bottomed saucepan. Cover and simmer gently for 5 minutes, then stir in the sugar and cook for 3–4 minutes more.

2 In a cup mix the arrowroot flour with the remaining water and stir into the cranberry mixture. Bring to a boil, lower the heat and simmer for 1–2 minutes until thick and no longer cloudy, stirring constantly.

3 Cool the cranberry mixture for 30 minutes, then taste and stir in more sugar if liked. Divide the mixture equally among 4 custard cups or other small heatproof dishes.

4 Preheat the broiler to hot.

5 Spread the sour cream over the cranberry mixture, almost to the edges. Mix the sugar and spice and sprinkle evenly on top of the cream.

6 Place under the broiler for a few seconds, until the sugar is melted and bubbling. Remove the creams from the heat, let them settle for a few minutes, then serve immediately.

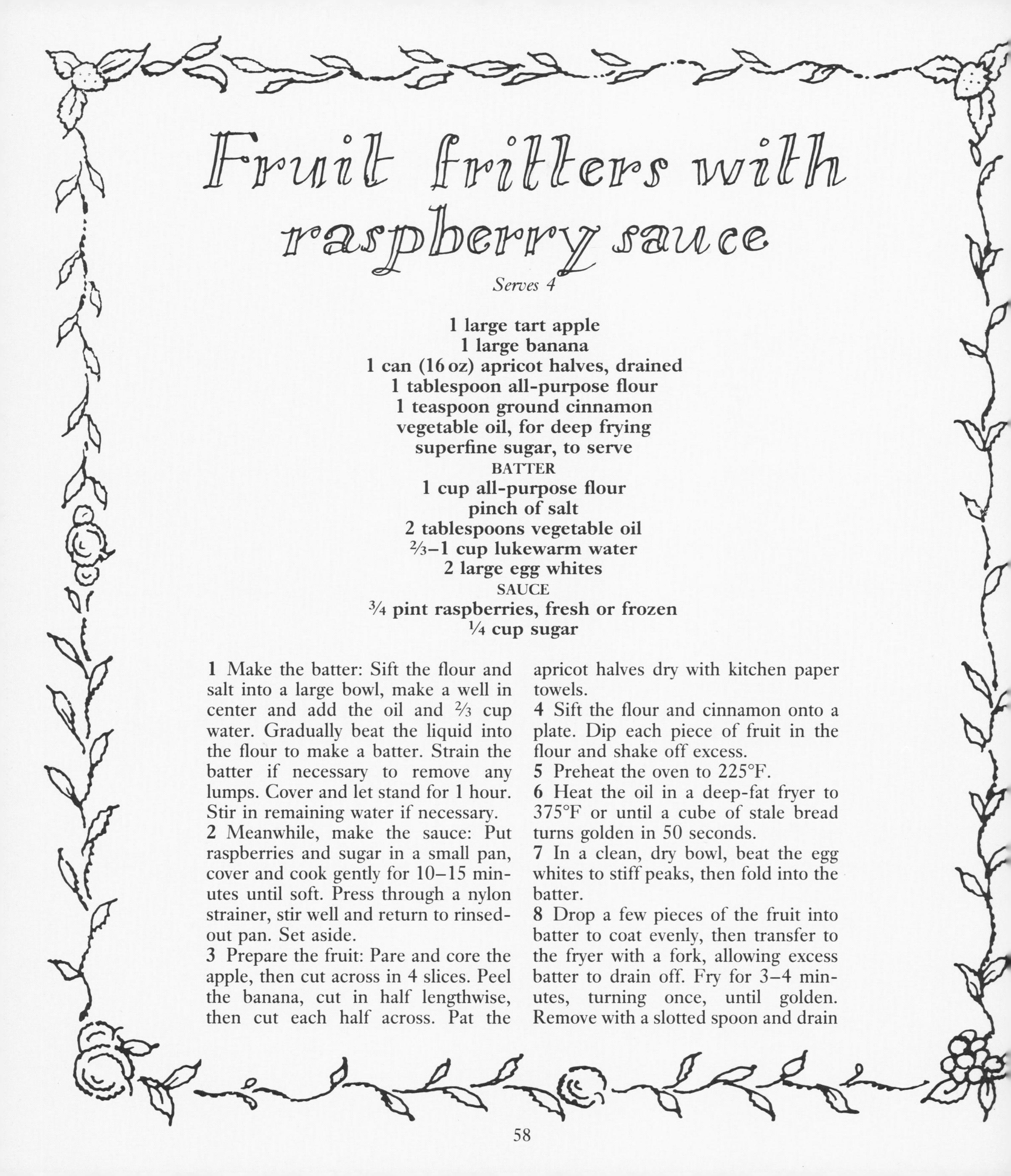

Fruit fritters with raspberry sauce

Serves 4

1 large tart apple
1 large banana
1 can (16 oz) apricot halves, drained
1 tablespoon all-purpose flour
1 teaspoon ground cinnamon
vegetable oil, for deep frying
superfine sugar, to serve

BATTER

1 cup all-purpose flour
pinch of salt
2 tablespoons vegetable oil
⅔–1 cup lukewarm water
2 large egg whites

SAUCE

¾ pint raspberries, fresh or frozen
¼ cup sugar

1 Make the batter: Sift the flour and salt into a large bowl, make a well in center and add the oil and ⅔ cup water. Gradually beat the liquid into the flour to make a batter. Strain the batter if necessary to remove any lumps. Cover and let stand for 1 hour. Stir in remaining water if necessary.

2 Meanwhile, make the sauce: Put raspberries and sugar in a small pan, cover and cook gently for 10–15 minutes until soft. Press through a nylon strainer, stir well and return to rinsed-out pan. Set aside.

3 Prepare the fruit: Pare and core the apple, then cut across in 4 slices. Peel the banana, cut in half lengthwise, then cut each half across. Pat the apricot halves dry with kitchen paper towels.

4 Sift the flour and cinnamon onto a plate. Dip each piece of fruit in the flour and shake off excess.

5 Preheat the oven to 225°F.

6 Heat the oil in a deep-fat fryer to 375°F or until a cube of stale bread turns golden in 50 seconds.

7 In a clean, dry bowl, beat the egg whites to stiff peaks, then fold into the batter.

8 Drop a few pieces of the fruit into batter to coat evenly, then transfer to the fryer with a fork, allowing excess batter to drain off. Fry for 3–4 minutes, turning once, until golden. Remove with a slotted spoon and drain on kitchen paper towels. Keep warm in the oven, while cooking remaining fruit.

9 To serve: Reheat the raspberry sauce and pour into a pitcher. Arrange the fritters on a warmed serving dish and sprinkle with the superfine sugar. Pour the raspberry sauce evenly over the top and serve at once, while the fritters are still warm.

Spiced peach compote

Serves 4

4 large firm peaches
little lemon juice, for brushing
¼ cup slivered almonds, toasted
light cream, to serve (optional)

SYRUP

⅔ cup water
¼ cup sugar
finely grated rind and juice of 1 orange
2 tablespoons currant jelly
small piece cinnamon stick
3 whole cloves

1 Cut the peaches in half and remove the pits, then brush the cut surfaces with lemon juice to prevent the flesh discoloring.

2 Make the syrup: Pour the water into a large heavy-bottomed pan and add the sugar, orange rind and juice, the currant jelly and spices. Heat gently, stirring, until the jelly has melted and sugar has dissolved, then bring the syrup mixture to a boil.

3 Using a slotted spoon, lower the peach halves into the syrup. Bring back to a boil, then lower the heat, cover and poach the peaches gently for 5–10 minutes, until just tender all the way through. Remove the pan of peaches from the heat.

4 Using a slotted spoon, transfer the peaches to a plate. Leave for a few minutes until cool enough to handle, then slip off the skins with your fingers. Place the peaches in a heat-proof serving bowl, then strain the hot syrup over them.

5 Serve the peaches warm, or chill in the refrigerator and serve cold. Scatter the almonds over the peaches just before serving. Pass a pitcher of cream separately, if liked.

Orange ice-cream cups

Serves 6

6 oranges
1¼ cups heavy cream
⅔ cup confectioners' sugar
finely grated rind of 1 orange (optional)
⅓ cup Grand Marnier
fresh bay leaves, for decoration (optional)

1 Cut a very thin slice off the bottom of each orange, if necessary, so it stands level, then cut a slice off the top to reserve as a lid. Carefully squeeze the juice from the oranges, taking care not to break the shells. Strain the juice into a liquid measure and reserve. Gently scrape out the remaining flesh and membranes and discard it. Rinse the outside of each orange shell and pat them dry.

2 Arrange the orange cases and "lids" on a baking sheet and place in the freezer or freezing compartment of the refrigerator while you make the orange liqueur cream mixture.

3 Pour the cream into a bowl. Add the sugar and rind, if using, and beat until thick and creamy. Slowly beat in the Grand Marnier and ⅔ cup of the strained orange juice and continue beating until the orange cream stands in soft peaks.

4 Divide the orange cream equally among the prepared orange shells. Return to the freezer (uncovered) for at least 8 hours or overnight until the mixture is firm.

5 To serve: Place each orange ice cream cup on a dessert plate and replace the lid. Decorate with bay leaves, if using, and serve at once.

Poached pears with butterscotch sauce

Serves 4

4 dessert pears, slightly underripe
1¼ cups water
2 tablespoons light corn syrup
3 inch cinnamon stick
1 strip of lemon rind
¼ cup finely chopped walnuts, to serve

SAUCE

⅓ cup packed light brown sugar
2 tablespoons light corn syrup
2 tablespoons butter
1 tablespoon lemon juice
1¼ cups heavy cream
2 egg yolks

1 Peel and core the pears from the bottom, using an apple corer. Put the water, corn syrup, cinnamon stick and lemon rind in a saucepan and set over a low heat until the syrup has melted.

2 Bring to the simmering point, add the pears and poach very gently until they are tender and transparent but still firm, about 30 minutes. Remove from the heat and let cool in the syrup.

3 Make the sauce: Put the brown sugar, syrup, butter and lemon juice into a saucepan. Set over a low heat until the mixture has melted. Remove the pan from the heat.

4 Pour the cream into a pan and bring it to just below the boiling point. Stir it into the sugar and syrup mixture.

5 Beat the egg yolks in a small bowl. Beat in about 6 tablespoons of the cream mixture, then stir this back into the pan. Set over a low heat and stir with a wooden spoon until it begins to thicken. Off heat, let the sauce cool completely.

6 To serve, remove the pears from the syrup with a slotted spoon and arrange them on a serving dish. Spoon the sauce over the top and decorate with the chopped walnuts.

Fresh fruit salad with honey cream

Serves 6

2 large oranges
juice of 1 lemon
1 cup halved and seeded purple grapes
2 large dessert pears
1 red-skinned dessert apple, preferably Cortland
½ melon
1 large banana

HONEY CREAM

1 package (3 oz) cream cheese
2 tablespoons milk
2 tablespoons honey
grated rind of 1 lemon
⅔ cup heavy cream

1 Make the honey cream: Soften the cheese in a bowl with a wooden spoon, then gradually beat in the milk, honey and lemon rind.

2 Whip the cream until thick but not stiff, then gradually whip in the cheese mixture. Cover the bowl and refrigerate the honey cream while preparing the fruit salad.

3 Using a sharp knife, peel the oranges thickly, taking care to remove every bit of white pith. Squeeze the peel with your fingers over a large bowl to extract any juice.

4 Divide the oranges in sections by cutting between the membranes. Remove any seeds. Cut the sections in half and place in the bowl with the lemon juice and grapes.

5 Peel, halve and core the pears; cut in cubes and mix with the orange sections and grapes. Halve and core, but do not pare, the apple; cut in cubes and mix with the other fruit.

6 Scrape out the seeds and membrane from the melon; scoop out the flesh with a melon baller and add to bowl.

7 Just before serving, peel and slice the banana and add to the bowl. Mix the fruit gently but thoroughly, then transfer to a serving bowl with a slotted spoon. Pass the cream separately.

Date & walnut baked apples

Serves 4

4 large tart apples, preferably Rome Beauty
⅓ cup natural unsweetened apple juice
whipped cream, to serve

FILLING

⅓ cup pitted dates, roughly chopped
1 tablespoon chopped walnuts
2 tablespoons light brown sugar
½ teaspoon ground cinnamon

1 Preheat the oven to 350°F.
2 Using an apple corer or a small sharp knife, remove the core from each apple. Score the skin around the center of each apple with a sharp knife.
3 Make the filling: Mix together the dates, walnuts, sugar and cinnamon in a bowl. Use to fill cavities, pressing down firmly with the back of a teaspoon.
4 Place in an ovenproof dish, then pour apple juice around apples.
5 Bake in oven for 50–60 minutes, basting occasionally with the apple juice, until the apples are soft when pierced with a sharp knife.
6 Serve at once, with whipped cream.

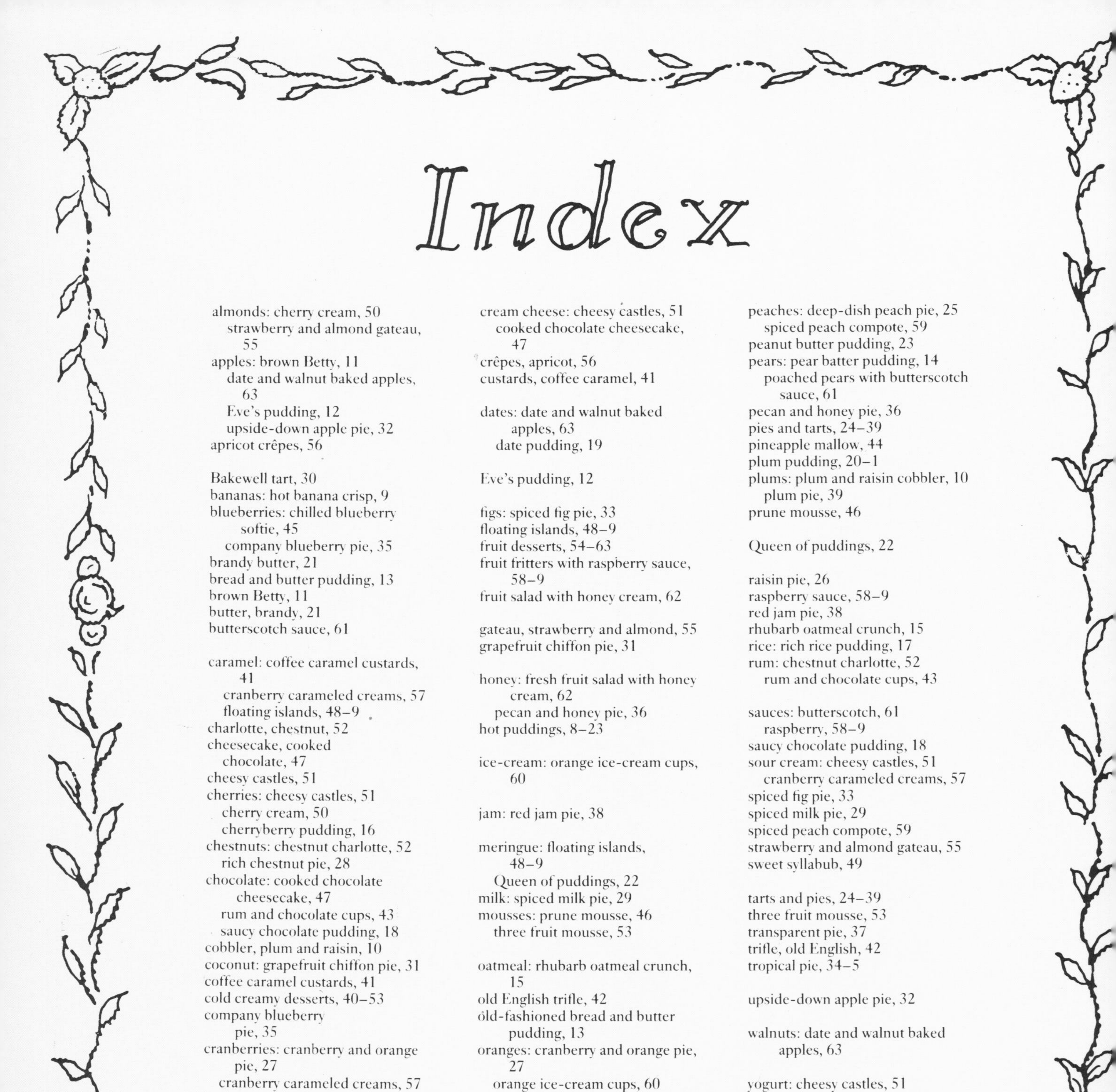

Index